Geographies of Media

Series Editors
Torsten Wissmann
Faculty of Architecture and Urban Planning
University of Applied Sciences
Erfurt, Germany

Joseph Palis
Department of Geography
University of the Philippines Diliman
Quezon, Philippines

Media is always spatial: spaces extend from all kinds of media, from news-paper columns to Facebook profiles, from global destination branding to individually experienced environments, and from classroom methods to GIS measurement techniques. Crucially, the way information is produced in an increasingly globalised world has resulted in the bridging of space between various scalar terrains. Being and engaging with media means being linked to people and places both within and beyond traditional political borders. As a result, media shapes and facilitates the formation of new geographies and other space-constituting and place-based configura-tions. The *Geographies of Media* series serves as a forum to engage with the shape-shifting dimensions of mediascapes from an array of method-ological, critical and analytical perspectives. The series welcomes proposals for monographs and edited volumes exploring the cultural and social impact of multi-modal media on the creation of space, place, and every-day life.

Ola Johansson
Séverin Guillard • Joseph Palis
Editors

New Geographies of Music 1

Urban Policies, Live Music, and Careers
in a Changing Industry

Editors
Ola Johansson
University of Pittsburgh at Johnstown
Johnstown, PA, USA

Séverin Guillard
University of Picardie Jules Verne
Amiens, France

Joseph Palis
Department of Geography
University of the Philippines Diliman
Quezon, Philippines

Geographies of Media
ISBN 978-981-99-0756-4   ISBN 978-981-99-0757-1   (eBook)
https://doi.org/10.1007/978-981-99-0757-1

This Palgrave Macmillan imprint is published by the registered company Springer Nature Singapore Pte Ltd.
The registered company address is: 152 Beach Road, #21-01/04 Gateway East, Singapore 189721, Singapore

SERIES EDITORS' PREFACE: BIGGER, BETTER, FASTER, MORE!

Welcome (back) to our *Geographies of Media* series. Like always, we want to connect authors, ideas, and readers using our most accessible Pivot format. Over the last few years, this series has focused on studies that all share a common core: media geography. The book you are about to read is no different, except it is.

If you follow our series, you know we try to cover a broad spectrum of media-related topics. But in between Boos' *Inhabiting cyberspace and emerging cyberplaces* (2017), Barns' *Platform urbanism* (2020), and the consumer drones in Hildebrand's *Aerial Play* (2022), there are two publications both of which focus on music as a medium. If you had a chance to pick up Johansson's *Songs from Sweden* (2021) or read about pirate radio stations in Peters' *Sound, space and society* (2018), you know that music is a subfield within media geography that contains an exceedingly wide variety of research topics.

As *Songs from Sweden* shows, traditional media, such as music, today use the potential of new (social) media connectivity to extend its production processes, marketing strategies, and artistic possibilities. Internet connectivity spreads across the globe and affects how we produce, experience, and communicate music. But even within a globalized music industry, localized networks and specific places are still of importance and add their unique qualities to the medium of music, as the example of Cheiron Studios in Stockholm shows (see Johansson, 2021, p. 45).

When Johansson, Guillard, and Palis (not a band name) approached us with the idea of highlighting the places where music affects our lives, we listened very closely. In addition to the interconnections of the global music industry, learning about local phenomena, performances, and processes is most significant to obtain a complete picture of the geographies of music.

Some cities tolerate live music as an attractive cultural touch, while others actively use the local music scene to develop urban quarters. City marketing sometimes even centers around the music industry to promote a specific place image (see Relph, 1976) and to create a unique brand (see Wissmann, 2014). Whether music is played in the streets or performed in concert halls, whether it is born in performative acts or crafted within a network of sound design specialists: music always (co-)creates both spaces and places.

Wouldn't it be a good idea to find all those topics in one place and get a chance to discover potential interconnections? But how should we do that? We could easily designate the upcoming fifteen volumes of our series to cover music-related media geographic research. Great idea, right?—No. We still want to pursue our overall goal to serve "as a forum to engage with the shape-shifting dimensions of [all] mediascapes. "So, maybe we should pick only the most compelling topics?—That doesn't seem fair. How should we determine which studies are most interesting to you?— This is where Johansson, Guillard, and Palis come into play. They introduced the idea of using the Pivot format to produce an edited trilogy about new geographies of music!

Thus, *Urban Policies, Live Music, and Careers in a Changing Industry* is the exciting first volume of our trilogy on the *New Geographies of Music 1*. It contains the first five specific chapters from different cities and different countries. Starting with *The Values of Live Music in Urban Development*, Arno van der Hoeven and Erik Hitters tell a story about the city of Rotterdam. Then, Ola Johansson's *The Music Cities Movement and Circulation of Best Practices* shifts the focus to Washington, D.C., with his intriguing analysis of how cities use music for marketing and identification. Crossing the Atlantic Ocean again, Kai Marquardt and Christoph Mager investigate the *Relational Geographies of the German Music Market*. Séverin Guillard subsequently takes us to Lille, France, and Atlanta, USA, to tell us about *Local Scenes, National Industry, and Virtual Platforms*. Finally, Adam Zendel dissolves music's localization to a specific city when he discusses the life of traveling musicians in *On the Road: Precarious Work and Life in the Live Music Industry*.

We hope you enjoy this first volume on the *New Geographies of Music 1* as much as we do. Subsequently, the second volume will investigate *Music in*

Urban Tourism, Heritage Politics, and Place-making. Finally, *Imagining Music and Places* will complete the trilogy as its third volume.

If I might add a general and more critical note to this preface, we are most excited to present you this collection on the *New Geographies of Music 1.* However, the current compilation cannot claim and won't claim to have captured the entirety of novel media geographic music-related research. With their selection, Johansson, Guillard, and Palis not only encourage us to listen more carefully to the variety of tunes emerging from the field. They also challenge us to encounter the complementary part of all sound: Its absence. Like John Cage's composition 4'33" (see Vanel, 2008) enriches our understanding of music, this trilogy actively points out the "lack of awareness from Anglophone researchers regarding the work produced in other languages." Although *Urban Policies, Live Music, and Careers in a Changing Industry* is in English, it consists of contributions from the USA, France, Germany, and the Netherlands.

As co-editor of the *Geographies of Media* series, I wonder about those absent tunes: How could our research benefit from media geographic studies from other disciplines, countries, and even continents? With this first volume on the *New Geographies of Music 1*, I would like to open up a critical debate on media geography. Therefore, I am calling for a more diverse group of researchers to enter the media geography discussion and contribute to our *Geographies of Media* series. I would like to read more about media-related research conducted in places never or only rarely covered before.

As for the *New Geographies of Music 1*: Johansson, Guillard, and Palis have listened to numerous presentations, talks, and discussions to compile the trilogy. Their final selection is genuinely impressive.

Or, as Joni Mitchell puts it: "We managed to put together a compilation that had some creativity to it."

Erfurt, Germany   Torsten Wissmann

REFERENCES

Barns, S. (2020). *Platform urbanism. Negotiating platform ecosystems in connected cities.* Palgrave Macmillan.

Boos, T. (2017). *Inhabiting cyberspace and emerging cyberplaces. The case of Siena, Italy.* Palgrave Macmillan.

Hildebrand, J. M. (2022). *Aerial play. Drone medium, mobility, communication, and culture*. Palgrave Macmillan.

Johansson, O. (2021). *Songs from Sweden. Shaping pop culture in a globalized music industry*. Palgrave Macmillan.

Peters, K. (2018). *Sound, space and society. Rebel radio*. Palgrave Macmillan.

Relph, E. C. (1976). *Place and placelessness*. Pion.

Vanel, H. (2008). John Cage's Muzak-Plus: The fu (rni) ture of music. *Representations, 102*(1), 94–128.

Wissmann, T. (2014). *Geographies of urban sound*. Ashgate.

CONTENTS

Notes on Contributors

Séverin Guillard is Assistant Professor in Geography at the University of Picardie Jules Verne (France), and a member of the research unit *Habiter le Monde* (Inhabiting the World). His research focuses on music and cultural policies and events in French, American, and British cities.

Erik Hitters is Associate Professor of Media and Creative Industries in the Department of Media & Communication of Erasmus University Rotterdam, the Netherlands. He has co-founded and is managing director of the Erasmus Research Centre for Media, Communication and Culture. Hitter's research interests lie in the broad field of transformations in the media and cultural industries.

Ola Johansson is Professor of Geography at the University of Pittsburgh at Johnstown, USA. He holds a PhD from the University of Tennessee. Johansson is author of the book *Songs from Sweden* (2020, Palgrave Macmillan), and co-author of *Sound, Society, and the Geography of Popular Music* and *World Regional Geography*.

Christoph Mager is a senior lecturer at the Institute of Geography and Geoecology, Karlsruhe Institute of Technology (KIT), Germany. His research interests include social and cultural geography, cultural infrastructures, and music and geography.

Kai Marquardt is a graduate student at the Karlsruhe Institute of Technology (KIT), Germany. His research interests include computer science education.

Joseph Palis is an associate professor and Chairperson at the Department of Geography, University of the Philippines Diliman. He has been a DJ at WXYC Chapel Hill since 2006.

Arno van der Hoeven is a visiting fellow in the Department of Media & Communication at Erasmus University Rotterdam, The Netherlands. He is also a project manager for Platform 31 in The Hague.

Adam Zendel is a PhD candidate at the Department of Geography and Planning and a researcher at the Cultural Economy Lab, University of Toronto, Canada. His research sits at the intersection of cultural, economic, and labor geographies.

LIST OF FIGURES

LIST OF TABLES

Introduction: Approaching the Spatiality of Popular Music Through Geographical and Interdisciplinary Perspectives

Ola Johansson, Séverin Guillard, and Joseph Palis

Abstract Over the last few decades, a rich body of literature has explored the importance of music to understand the spatial dimensions of society. These geographic approaches to music are varied, depending on the background of the researchers. While music has generated a substantial interest among geographers, scholars in other disciplines have also developed related spatial perspectives on music. These multiple approaches to the

O. Johansson (✉)
University of Pittsburgh at Johnstown, Johnstown, PA, USA
e-mail: johans@pitt.edu

S. Guillard
University of Picardie Jules Verne, Amiens, France
e-mail: severin.guillard@u-picardie.fr

J. Palis
Department of Geography, University of the Philippines Diliman,
Quezon City, Philippines
e-mail: jepalis@up.edu.ph

© The Author(s), under exclusive license to Springer Nature   1
Singapore Pte Ltd. 2023
O. Johansson et al. (eds.), *New Geographies of Music 1*, Geographies
of Media, https://doi.org/10.1007/978-981-99-0757-1_1

geographies of popular music are the ones that our book series bring together. This volume is the first installment of a three-part book series, *New Geographies of Music*. In this chapter, we will explore these perspectives, discuss how they provide a multitude of lenses through which we can study of popular music, and investigate how the five chapters in this book contribute to the advancement of music geography.

Keywords Music geographies • Popular music • Interdisciplinary study of music • Cultural geography • Spatiality in music

Over the last few decades, a rich body of literature has explored the importance of music to understand the spatial dimensions of society. These geographic approaches to music are varied, depending on the background of the researchers. While music has generated a substantial interest among geographers, scholars in other disciplines have also developed related spatial perspectives on music. These multiple approaches to the geographies of popular music are the ones that our book series bring together. This volume is the first installment of a three-part book series, *New Geographies of Music*. In this chapter, we will explore these perspectives, discuss how they provide a multitude of lenses through which we can study of popular music, and investigate how the five chapters in this book contribute to the advancement of music geography.

1   THE GEOGRAPHIES OF MUSIC: UNDERSTANDING THE ROLE OF MUSIC IN THE CONSTRUCTION OF SPACE AND PLACE

During recent decades, music has become a legitimate object of analysis among geographers. While some pioneering works on music and sound go back to the 1920s (Cornish, 1928) the first comprehensive wave of works occurred in the 1970s (e.g. Ford, 1971; Carney, 1978) This early music geography investigated the place of music in local, national, and global contexts; the relationship between soundscapes and specific places; the diffusion and distribution of musical styles; and geographical imagery in lyrics (see Leyshon et al., 1995).

While the study of music was situated at the margins of the discipline for some time, its position strengthened in the 1990s and 2000s. This evolution was part of broader changes in geography where a "cultural turn" led many researchers toward an interest in cultural, creative, and artistic practices (Aitken & Valentine, 2009). The cultural turn transformed the study of music as a new generation of geographers adopted a variety of new approaches. Several seminal publications published at that time argued that the geography of music is more than highlighting the sites where music is produced (or diffused from) or about places mentioned in songs. It is also about how spatiality—a socially constructed geography—plays a role in the formation and creation of music, and how it reflects "mutually generative relations of music and place" (Leyshon et al., 1995, p. 425).

Building on that momentum, the geography of music has continued to contribute to the discipline at large. In particular, a new interest regarding the role of sound as part of bodily, physical experiences has challenged a discipline often focused on visual dimensions and representations (Bonner-Thompson & Hopkins, 2017). Other works have also illustrated how music can build links between academic geographers and artists and practitioners (see, e.g., Hracs et al., 2016 and Zendel in this volume). In the book *Sound Tracks*, Connell and Gibson (2003) proposed ways to overcome the global/local dichotomy often used in conceptualizing globalization, arguing that, in music, both spatial manifestations take place at the same time. They suggested instead the concepts of fluidity and fixity as central to understanding the spatiality of musical practices. That is, how music is always mobile and thus subject to change as it moves across space, while it is also shaped by local forces and becomes fixed in place.

Moreover, geographers became interested in adopting a spatial lens to understand musical practices that until then had mostly been within the purview of other disciplines. In particular, geographical perspectives reexamined all dimensions of music practices, from production and consumption (Hracs et al., 2016), to local music cultures (Kong, 1995), and the global reach of the mainstream music industry (Connell & Gibson, 2003). In doing so, music geographers are not always making a strict distinction between popular music and other musical forms. In various publications, popular music has been studied alongside classical music (Leyshon et al., 1995), folk music (Revill & Gold, 2018), and within the context of a broader geography of sounds (Anderson et al., 2005; Wissmann, 2014).

Reading the work of music geographers, it is evident that not all studies can be subsumed under one single theoretical umbrella. As Johansson and Bell (2009) explain it, there are "multiple perspectives on the relationships among music and geography; perspectives that are eclectic in terms of research methodology and underlying philosophy" (p. 2). This has sometimes been linked to the nature of musical activity in itself, which "cannot be contained with a single explanatory theory" as music culture is "dynamic and unpredictable, involving movements of sounds and people, expressing mobility in certain period, stability in others" (Connell & Gibson, 2003, p. 17). The result is a sense that music geography research has not led to the emergence of an overarching theory, given that "there are as many musical geographies as there are geographers" (Guiu, 2006). This fragmentation has been accentuated by a lack of awareness from Anglophone researchers regarding the work produced in other languages, despite the rise of significant research in for example French, Italian, and Spanish (Guiu, 2006; Canova, 2014; dell'Agnese, 2019; dell'Agnese & Tabusi, 2016; Dozena, 2016; Panitz, 2012). While researchers in the non-Anglophone world often cite work produced in English, the contrary is rarely true, despite the fact that some of these publications propose innovative theoretical perspectives for the discipline, grounded in their national disciplinary debates (see e.g., a discussion on the idea of "territory" in Canova, 2013).

Therefore, rather than arriving at a common approach, music geographers have pursued various theoretical strains developed within the discipline, following the evolutions of multiple debates. In particular, but without intending to be exhaustive, we want to mention three important (and interrelated) perspectives. In relation to social and cultural geography, the study of music has evolved from an emphasis on lyrics as the carrier of meaning (Leyshon et al., 1995) to a focus on musical practices and performances, in the context of broader calls in the discipline for approaching the world as lived and embodied rather than just represented (Wood et al., 2007; Anderson & Harrison, 2016). More recently, works have also unveiled the material culture of musical objects, for example through the production of instruments such as guitars (Gibson & Warren, 2021). The study of economic music geography has also made an important contribution. This includes seminal works using music to explore creative economy clustering (Scott, 1999; Florida & Jackson, 2010; Watson, 2008), studies addressing the music industry through the circulation of music production and songs in globalized networks (Johansson, 2020), the impact of digital technology (Leyshon, 2014; Hracs et al., 2016), the nature of work within the confined space of the studio (Watson, 2014), and the entrepreneurial strategies of musicians (Mbaye, 2011). Finally, the perspectives of urban geography have also been crucial. In addition to studies that explore how music conveys geographical imaginaries of urban environments

(Guillard, 2016), a wave of public policies aiming to attract and promote creativity has generated scholarly interest in analyzing the impacts of music-led urban (re)development policies (Ballico & Watson, 2020). Here, music geographers have been at the forefront of contextualizing and critiquing the idea of the "creative city" (Florida, 2002), while also providing critical accounts regarding the way music is used to reinforce the city's attractiveness in the context of global inter-urban competition.

2   UNDERSTANDING THE SPATIAL DIMENSION OF MUSIC WORLDS BEYOND THE DISCIPLINE OF GEOGRAPHY

Far from being limited to geography, research on the spatial dimensions of music has also been carried out in other fields of study. Such approaches have been quite diverse, adopted by researchers in musicology (Krims, 2007; Whiteley et al., 2004), anthropology (Stokes, 1997), sociology (Holt & Wergin, 2013; Bennett, 2000), and media studies (Stahl & Percival, 2022). In many cases, they are linked to a renewed interest in space and place initiated by a geographical turn (Straw quoted in Janotti Jr., 2012) in many disciplines during the 1990s and 2000s. While some of these studies exhibit familiarity with the debates in geography, most of them approached the spatial dimension of musical practices using theoretical models and discussions of their own discipline. This has led to approaches which, while addressing concerns that are close to the perspective of geographers, have often emerged independently, and do not necessarily engage in a dialog with geographic research.

This observation is also true of interdisciplinary fields specifically dedicated to the study of music. The 1980s saw the emergence of popular music studies and since the 1990s, many researchers in this field have highlighted the importance of the spatial dimension of music. While geographers have mainly been interested in the role of music in the production of space and place, popular music studies address spatiality through songs and music practices. This led to the rise of theoretical models distinct from the ones mobilized by music geographers; in particular, studies focused on music genres as sites of production for geographical imaginaries that evolved through time and at the intersection of race, class, and gender (Peterson, 1997; Forman, 2002). Embedded in these studies was also a discussion around space as a crucial dimension in the construction of "authenticity" within music genres. Other works focused more on the contexts of music activities, mainly through the emergence of "scenes," an idea which has generated important debates about the geographies of artistic worlds, and ways of approaching the concept theoretically and empirically (Straw, 1991; Bennett & Peterson, 2004; Kruse, 2003; Woo et al., 2015; Guibert & Bellavance, 2014). More recently, these issues are also analyzed through the "ecology" of local music (see, e.g., Van der Hoeven et al., 2020). Much like the concept of scene, ecology emphasizes the rooting of music actors in a broader environment. The music ecosystem concept, though, bridges the dichotomy of music industry and scenes by incorporating people, entities, and structures often excluded from how both music industry and scenes are usually conceptualized (Behr et al., 2016). Concrete ecology is also addressed in ecomusicology, an interdisciplinary endeavor that emerged in the 2000s, which "considers the relationships of music, culture, and nature; i.e., it is the study of musical and sonic issues, both textual and performative, as they relate to ecology and the environment" (Allen, 2011, p. 392). Despite the centrality of nature-society interaction in geography, ecomusicology has yet to penetrate the discipline, with precious few exceptions (Tyner et al., 2016).

3   THE INCREASING HYBRIDIZATION OF THE STUDY OF SPACE AND MUSIC

We should acknowledge that the analyses of music carried out in geography and in other fields of study have not always been disconnected from each other. Reading the literature in geography, we notice references to spatial approaches developed elsewhere. For example, Leyshon et al. (1995) ground their work in cultural and media studies (from historical figures like Theodor Adorno to contemporary scholars like Will Straw) while Connell and Gibson (2003) cover the debates and approaches developed in popular music studies, such as scenes and authenticity. Similarly, Johansson and Bell (2009) build on work that address geographical features of popular music, but not necessarily originating in geography. Reverse quotations can also be found by researchers in other disciplines. Popular music studies have mobilized the theoretical background developed in geography, from the cultural and social approaches of Edward Soja to the Marxist perspective on the organization and evolution of the American city by David Harvey, or the work on youth cultures by Skelton and Valentine (Forman, 2002; Krims, 2007; Stahl, 2004).

While debates have remained somewhat compartmentalized, trends of cross-fertilization are evident within and outside geography. For example, musicology has embraced social and cultural theory and geographers have moved from a focus on the extra-musical to music in itself, in order to understand "what music and sound do rather that what either represents" (Anderson et al., 2005, p. 640). Thus, a sensible evolution can be noticed, as recent research shows an increased hybridization of approaches that were originally separate. For example, there is interdisciplinary hybridization on issues relating to scenes and urban/tourism policies (Bolderman, 2020), or the emergence of networks such as the urban music scholars' network (see urbanmusicstudies.org) which aims to gather scholars from various backgrounds. This also reflected in that Palgrave Pivot's Geographies of Media books are not just written by geographers, an initiative that aims to foster encounters between geographers and researchers in other disciplines. Therefore, while Johansson and Bell concluded in 2009 that there was no recent edited volume on music geography, now there are an increasing number of books that are dealing with one or several aspects of music/space/place relationships, though they are not always written by geographers (Baker, 2019; Ballico, 2021; Stahl & Percival, 2022).

With increasing production, growing hybridization of research, but also intellectual fragmentation by subtheme, one may wonder if there is still a need for a series of edited books dedicated to music geography. We think that such initiative is important for several reasons:

- It contributes to the coherence of the discussion on music, space, and place, as well as to the dialog between the perspectives developed by geographers and those that have emerged in other disciplines;
- It highlights emerging as well as established avenues of research in music geography, through the work of researchers who are actively engaged in these debates and/or bring new perspectives to them;
- And it covers theoretical perspectives on the evolving relationship between music, space and place, as well as introducing new empirical case studies.

This book series is the result of an effort during the past few years to generate a dialog among researchers interested in music geography. In particular, it evolved from multiple paper sessions that gathered more than 30 scholars, organized at the American Association of Geographers (AAG) annual meetings. While paying attention to the legacy of music, space, and place, this book series also expands into new directions. To this end, the *New Geographies of Music* reflect contemporary music research, whether shedding light on increasingly significant aspects of this topic, or developing new theoretical and methodological perspectives.

While previous edited collections on music geography adopted the format of a single book or a journal issue aiming to encompass multiple dimensions, we have decided to publish three Palgrave Pivot monographs oriented around separate but related perspectives. While recognizing that the growth of research on the geographies of music may lead to atomization around specific subthemes, it is also important to maintain a common conversation. Therefore, we decided to design our series as three books where each explores a bundle of interrelated themes so the reader has the option focus on one set of issues or, more expansively (which is preferable), read all three.

Obviously, *New Geographies of Music* does not intend to cover the full spectrum of research in music geography, as it is dependent on the topics and case studies chosen by individual chapter authors. Yet, we hope that it can provide a way for researchers to navigate a multitude of discourses at the intersection of music and geography, as well as to provide a basis for further development of the field.

4   THE CONTENT OF *NEW GEOGRAPHIES OF MUSIC 1*

The background to this first installment of *New Geographies of Music* is that the music industry has undergone important changes related to the crisis of the recording industry and the rise of online consumption of music. This has led to a reorganization of the music sector, including a growing importance of the live music business and a reconfiguration of the artists' career strategies. Following new research on the role of technology in the cultural, urban, and economic geographies of music (Leyshon, 2014; Hracs et al., 2016), the chapters in this book explore these new changes and their consequences.

One area of research is the role music plays in urban development. Since early baseline research on the topic (Krims, 2007), cities increasingly view local music scenes and the existence of a live music ecology as tools of economic development that create value for cities, often intending for them to appear as creative places in order to reinforce their attractiveness (Florida & Jackson, 2010). At the same time, as cities are gentrifying, live music venues often find themselves outcompeted and outregulated in favor of other land uses. As live music provides broader values to the city, closure of venues is a planning challenge for many urban areas. Other on-the-ground local struggles and transformations include corporatization (often of live music) versus local interests, and new digital music industry actors versus traditional industry actors. Not all of this takes place within cities but also in spatial networks, as with touring artists who for economic reasons face intensified pressure to be "on the road" and inter-urban connections in music recordings. In this book, we will present case studies that explore these issues.

The second chapter, "The Values of Live Music in Urban Development: The Case of Rotterdam," by Arno van der Hoeven and Erik Hitters examines the role of live music ecologies in urban development by distinguishing four different values. The social value of live music concerns its contribution to social capital, community engagement, and identity building in cities. Cultural value, which could also be described as the intrinsic value of music, encompasses the dimensions of musical creativity, cultural vibrancy, and talent development. The economic value of live music includes its role in job creation, increased tourism, and consumer spending. Finally, spatial value concerns the impact that live music has on the ways in which the physical environment of cities is experienced by citizens and managed by policy makers and urban planners. These values are explained by discussing the case of live music in Rotterdam in the Netherlands.

The subsequent chapter, "The Music Cities Movement and Circulation of Best Practices," by Ola Johansson changes location to the United States where cities, much like in Europe, want a thriving music ecosystem. The reasons are multifold; the music industry plays a role in the local economy, music is an important community-enhancing activity, and educated workers that cities want to recruit are looking for exciting and cosmopolitan cities in which to live and work. These objectives have spurred a music cities movement where previous fragmented policies toward local music are increasingly replaced by a comprehensive approach among urban stakeholders. How and where do new ideas about music and cities take shape and circulate? Johansson focuses on one such "microspace"—the Music Policy Forum—where non-profits, city officials, the music industry, and others share best practices. Through a participant observation of the 2019 Music Policy Forum, Johansson reveals a series of music and urban/economic/community development discourses that focused on organizational questions, strategy formation, funding opportunities and limitations, and on-the-ground challenges in the urban landscape.

In Chap. 4, "Centrality and Power in Urban Networks of Music Production: Exploring Relational Geographies of the German Music Market," Kai Marquardt and Christoph Mager explains how popular music emerges from production networks, in which various institutions and highly specialized actors such as musicians, producers, and sound engineers interact. As places where these actors come together, recording studios act as centers of musical creativity. Virtual and physical movements between recording studios then link cities around the world, forming urban networks of music production. Marquardt and Mager identify key cities of music production for the German music market in terms of their centrality, their power, and their position in global networks of music production. The chapter uses a social network analysis approach to scrutinize the urban production networks, which reveals new relational geographies of music production.

Another perspective on musical hierarchies is Séverin Guillard's "Local Scenes, National Industry, and Virtual Platforms: Overcoming Spatial Hierarchies in French and American Rap Music (2000–2015)." He argues in Chap. 5 that music practices are structured by spatial hierarchies between cores and peripheries. Scholars have previously addressed this issue through two main perspectives: irregular distribution of music infrastructures on a national scale, and local music scenes where "authenticity" of a genre is defined in a localized context. However, less is known about how hierarchies among music scenes are perpetuated, how artists are influenced by these hierarchies, and how they can overcome them to build their careers. In this chapter, Guillard addresses these issues by analyzing the evolving role of local rap scenes in United States (Atlanta) and France (Lille). He suggests that Lille and Atlanta provide a unique lens to highlight the power relations which influence artists' careers, and how they are reconfigured with the rise of new digital resources.

And finally, in "On the Road: Precarious Work and Life in the Live Music Industry," Adam Zendel explores how musicians increasingly rely on touring and live performance in order to earn a living. Drawing on 30 interviews with musicians and their crews, this chapter explores the working and living conditions of touring in the new music industry. While capital in the music industry has largely recovered from the crisis of piracy, musicians face new challenges. Touring has enabled many to survive in the industry, but it exposes musicians to new forms of risk and precarity.

Zendel's research finds that in order to tour, one must organize all aspects of life to be mobile. Touring is immediately precarious, as workers are exposed to the dangers of driving and stage work. While the fun and excitement of travel can be alluring, many describe that as the most exhausting part of touring. Life on tour is defined by the emotional highs of performing coupled with the drudgery of constant long-distance travel, the prevalence of drugs and alcohol, and distance from family and support networks. Touring can strain relationships both on and off the road. These problems fester into mental health issues, substance abuse, and burnout. This chapter links the recent transformation of the music industry with an increased pressure to tour and how this pressure shapes subjects and excludes others, how touring musicians and crew survive in this new music industry, and what this might mean for the future of the geography of music.

References

Aitken, S., & Valentine, G. (2009). *Approaches to human geography.* Sage.

Allen, A. (2011). Ecomusicology: Ecocriticism and musicology. *Journal of the American Musicological Society, 64*(2), 391–394.

Anderson, B., & Harrison, P. (2016). *Taking-place: Non-representational theories and geography.* Routledge.

Anderson, B., Morton, F., & Revill, G. (Eds.). (2005). Practice of music and sound. *Social & Cultural Geography, 6*(5), 639–644.

Baker, A. J. (2019). *The great music city: Exploring music, space and identity.* Palgrave Macmillan.

Ballico, C. (Ed.). (2021). *Geographically isolated and peripheral music scenes: Global insights and perspectives.* Palgrave Macmillan.

Ballico, C., & Watson, A. (Eds.). (2020). *Music cities. Evaluating a global cultural policy concept.* Palgrave Macmillan.

Behr, A., Brennan, M., Cloonan, M., Frith, S., & Webster, E. (2016). Live concert performance – An ecological approach. *Rock Music Studies, 3,* 5–23.

Bennett, A. (2000). *Popular music and youth culture: Music identity and place.* Macmillan.

Bennett, A., & Peterson, R. (2004). *Music scenes: Local, translocal and virtual.* Vanderbilt University Press.

Bolderman, L. (2020). *Contemporary music tourism: A theory of musical topophilia.* Routledge.

Bonner-Thompson, C., & Hopkins, P. (2017). *Geographies of the body.* Oxford University Press.

Canova, N. (2013). Music in French geography as space marker and placer maker. *Social & Cultural Geography, 14*(8), 861–867.

Canova, N. (2014). *La Musique au coeur de l'analyse géographique*. L'Harmattan.

Carney, G. (Ed.). (1978). *The sounds of people and places*. University Press of America.

Connell, J., & Gibson, C. (2003). *Sound tracks, popular music, identity and place*. Routledge.

Cornish, V. (1928). Harmonies of scenery: An outline of aesthetic geography. *Geography, 14*(275–282), 383–339.

dell'Agnese, E. (2019). *Musica (popolare) e spazi urbani: una introduzione*. Rivista Geografica Italiana. https://www.francoangeli.it/riviste/Scheda_rivista. aspx?IDArticolo=65196

dell'Agnese, E., & Tabusi, M. (Eds.). (2016). *La musica come geografia: suoni, luoghi, territori*. Società Geografica Italiana. http://societageografica.net/wp/ wp-content/uploads/2016/09/La_musica_come_geografia_ebook.pdf

Dozena, A. (Ed.). (2016). *Geografia e Música. Diálogos*. Edufrn.

Florida, R. (2002). *The rise of the creative class: And how it's transforming work, leisure, community and everyday life*. Basic Books.

Florida, R., & Jackson, S. (2010). Sonic city: The evolving economic geography of the music industry. *Journal of Planning Education and Research, 29*(3), 310–321.

Ford, L. (1971). Geographic factors in the origin, evolution, and diffusion of rock and roll music. *Journal of Geography, 70*(8), 455–464.

Forman, M. (2002). *The hood comes first: Race, space and place in rap and hip-hop*. Wesleyan.

Gibson, C., & Warren, A. (2021). *The guitar. Tracing the grain back to the tree*. University of Chicago Press.

Guibert, G., & Bellavance, G. (Eds.). (2014). La notion de "scène", entre sociologie de la culture et sociologie urbaine: génèse, actualité et perspectives. *Cahiers de la recherche sociologique, 57*, 5–180.

Guillard, S. (2016). *Musique, ville et scènes. Localisation et production de l'authenticité dans le rap en France et aux Etats-Unis*. Doctoral thesis, Université Paris Est.

Guiu, C. (2006). *Géographie et Musique, quelles perspectives?* Géographie et Cultures, n°59. L'Harmattan.

Holt, F., & Wergin, C. (2013). *Musical performance and the changing city. Postindustrial contexts in Europe and the United States*. Routledge.

Hracs, B., Seman, M., & Virani, T. (2016). *The production and consumption of music in the digital age*. Routledge.

Janotti, J., Jr. (2012). Interview – Will Straw and the importance of music scenes in music and communication studies. *Revista de Associação National dos Programas de Pos-Graduação, 15*(2).

Johansson, O. (2020). *Songs from Sweden. Shaping pop culture in a globalized music industry.* Palgrave Macmillan.

Johansson, O., & Bell, T. (2009). *Sound, society and the geography of popular music.* Ashgate.

Kong, L. (1995). Popular music and a "sense of place" in Singapore. *Crossroads, 9*(2), 51–77.

Krims, A. (2007). *Music and urban geography.* Routledge.

Kruse, H. (2003). *Site and sound: Understanding independent music scenes.* Peter Lang.

Leyshon, A. (2014). *Reformatted: Code, networks, and the transformation of the music industry.* Oxford University Press.

Leyshon, A., Matless, D., & Revill, G. (1995). The place of music [Introduction]. *Transactions of the Institute of British Geographers, 20*(4), 423–433.

Mbaye, J. (2011). *Reconsidering cultural entrepreneurship: Hip hop music economy and social change in Senegal, francophone West Africa.* Doctoral thesis, The London School of Economics and Political Science (LSE).

Panitz, L. (2012). Geografia e música: uma introdução ao tema. *Biblio3W. Revista bibliográfica de geografia y ciencias sociales, XVII*(978). http://www.ub.edu/geocrit/b3w-978.htm

Peterson, R. (1997). *Creating country music, Fabricating authenticity.* University of Chicago Press.

Revill, G., & Gold, J. R. (2018). "Far back in American time": Culture, region, nation, Appalachia, and the geography of voice. *Annals of the American Association of Geographers, 108*(5), 1406–1421.

Scott, A. J. (1999). The US recorded music industry: On the relations between organization, location, and creativity in the cultural economy. *Environment and Planning A, 31*, 1965–1984.

Stahl, G. (2004). It's like Canada reduced. Setting the scene in Montreal. In A. Bennett & K. Kahn-Harris (Eds.), *After subculture* (pp. 51–56). Palgrave Macmillan.

Stahl, G., & Percival, M. (2022). *The Bloomsbury handbook of popular music, space and place.* Bloomsbury.

Stokes, M. (1997). *Ethnicity, identity and music: The musical construction of place.* Berg.

Straw, W. (1991). System of articulation and logic of change: Communities and scenes in popular music. *Cultural Studies, 5*(3), 368–388.

Tyner, J., Rhodes, M., & Kimsroy, S. (2016). Music, nature, power, and place: An ecomusicology of Khmer Rouge songs. *GeoHumanities, 2*(2), 395–412.

Van der Hoeven, A., Hitters, E., Berkers, P., Mulder, M., & Everts, R. (2020). Theorizing the production and consumption of live music. A critical review. In E. Marzierska, L. Gillon, & T. Rigg (Eds.), *The future of music* (pp. 19–33). Bloomsbury Publishing.

Watson, A. (2008). Global music city: Knowledge and geographical proximity in London's recorded music industry. *Area, 40*(1), 12–23.

Watson, A. (2014). *Cultural production in and beyond the recording studio.* Routledge.

Whiteley, S., Bennett, A., & Hawkins, S. (2004). *Music, space and place: Popular music and cultural identity.* Routledge.

Wissmann, T. (2014). *Geographies of urban sound.* Ashgate.

Woo, B., Rennie, J., & Poyntz, S. (Eds.). (2015). Scene thinking. *Cultural Studies, 29*(3), 285–297.

Wood, N., Duffy, M., & Smith, S. (2007). The art of doing (geographies of) music. *Environment and Planning D: Society and Space, 25*(5), 867–889.

CHAPTER 2

The Values of Live Music in Urban Development: The Case of Rotterdam

Arno van der Hoeven and Erik Hitters

Abstract This chapter examines the values of live music in urban development. It builds on growing attention in research and policymaking to the role of live music in processes of urban change. We use the city of Rotterdam as a case study. Rotterdam is the second city of the Netherlands, known as a super-diverse port city with a long tradition of using cultural events to achieve various economic, social, and spatial objectives. The analysis of this case results in three theoretical contributions to the existing literature on the role of live music in urban planning. First, we discuss four different values of live music (i.e., economic, cultural, social, and spatial), which allow us to analyze the impact live music can have on cities. Second, we demonstrate the role of local specificities in how the values are achieved, as there is a level of path dependency in local policymaking and cultural production. Third, we highlight how these local dynamics need to be understood in connection to national and international developments.

A. van der Hoeven (✉) • E. Hitters
Department of Media & Communication, Erasmus University Rotterdam, Rotterdam, The Netherlands
e-mail: vanderhoeven@eshcc.eur.nl; hitters@eshcc.eur.nl

© The Author(s), under exclusive license to Springer Nature Singapore Pte Ltd. 2023
O. Johansson et al. (eds.), *New Geographies of Music 1*, Geographies of Media, https://doi.org/10.1007/978-981-99-0757-1_2

Policies aimed at furthering live music for urban development are embedded in national and international contexts of actors, policies, markets, and the transformation thereof.

Keywords Live music • Urban development • Popular music • Cultural policy • Values

1   INTRODUCTION

This chapter examines the values of live music in urban development by using the city of Rotterdam as a case study. It builds on growing attention in research and policymaking to the role of live music in processes of urban change (Kronenburg, 2020; Van der Hoeven & Hitters, 2020b). We understand live music as "events that bring musicians and audiences together in one place at one time and involve performance on vocals or other music instruments and technologies, or with music recordings" (Cohen, 2012, p. 587). As we will demonstrate in this chapter, these events can be used to achieve economic, cultural, social, and spatial values for urban spaces. Put succinctly, these values concern the benefits that live music has for cities and their inhabitants. However, it should be acknowledged that live music can also have unintentional negative effects, such as noise nuisance, unavailability of public spaces during festivals (e.g., parks), and damage to the flora and fauna in parks. Furthermore, gentrification is a key issue, as live music can make a neighborhood more attractive, while at the same time venues may suffer from rising rents and noise nuisance complaints from new neighbors (Van der Hoeven & Hitters, 2020a; Lobato, 2006).

The Dutch city of Rotterdam is an interesting case to study how live music is used in urban development. Rotterdam is the second city of the Netherlands, known as a super-diverse port city that hosts more than 180 different nationalities (Scholten et al., 2019; Swartjes & Berkers, 2022). Ever since the city was bombed during the Second World War and its cultural infrastructure largely destroyed, culture and the arts have been used in the urban reconstruction and economic development of the city. Especially festivals have played an important role in cultural provision. This makes it a relevant case to investigate the mix of festivals and bricks-and-mortar venues, as existing research on live music often has a bias toward the latter (Mulder et al., 2020). Furthermore, since Rotterdam struggles with high levels of social inequality, cultural events are increasingly expected to address issues of inclusivity in this city. This allows us to study how live music is connected to a range of socio-spatial issues.

The analysis of the case of Rotterdam is used to make three theoretical contributions to the existing literature on the role of live music in urban planning. First, we aim to distinguish four different values of live music (i.e., economic, cultural, social, and spatial), which allow us to analyze the impact live music can have on cities. Second, we demonstrate the role of local specificities in how the values are achieved, as there is a level of path dependency in local policymaking and cultural production. Third, we highlight how these local dynamics need to be understood in connection to national and international developments, including global policy approaches such as the music city concept (Bennett, 2020) and transformations in the global music industries (Holt, 2010).

This chapter begins by introducing the existing research on the connections between live music and urban spaces. It will then go on to describe our case study Rotterdam and analyze how live music is valued in this city. In doing so, we draw on research conducted in the context of the research project "Staging Popular Music: Researching Sustainable Live Music Ecologies for Artists, Music Venues and Cities" (POPLIVE). As part of this research, we analyzed policy-documents and conducted interviews with festival organizers, venue owners, and real estate experts.

2 Research on Live Music and Cities

Over the last decades, researchers have paid ample attention to processes of music-making and consumption in cities. For example, theoretical concepts like scenes, neo-tribes, and subcultures analyze the locally embedded social contexts in which live music is produced and consumed (Van der Hoeven et al., 2020). These approaches have been supplemented with research on (live) music activities that focuses on the city-level specifically. An example of this is the music city concept, which follows on from both the official UNESCO "Cities of Music" designation and an international approach to policymaking (Bennett, 2020; see also Johansson in this volume). Ballico and Watson (2020) distinguish "music cities" from scenes by stressing how music is actively used to achieve various social, economic, and cultural objectives:

We would suggest that the point of difference between music scenes and a 'Music City' is that in the case of the latter the city's music activity is supported, leveraged and activated beyond its music scene and industry functions. To this end, music is recognised by urban policy makers for its legacy and heritage, its ability to contribute to the cultural and creative identity of the city and as a driver for tourism and for economic growth. As a result, music is supported through a range of policy and funding initiatives, while also forming a vital component of city branding and place activation strategies. (p. 3)

A second example of a theoretical approach to live music that generally takes cities as the starting point is the concept of (urban) live music ecologies. This approach focuses on the local network of stakeholders in and outside the live music sector that enable music performances (Behr et al., 2016; Van der Hoeven et al., 2020). We draw on the live music ecology concept in this chapter to understand how a range of interrelated actors seeks to achieve economic, cultural, social, and spatial values. According to Behr et al. (2016), this concept highlights the materiality of the buildings where concerts take place, underscores the negotiation needed with actors outside the music sector (e.g., regulators), and allows an analysis of how local music cultures can be sustained. Furthermore, in this chapter we use the concept to understand the connections between local, national, and international developments in policymaking and the music industries. A live music ecology is shaped around a dynamic interplay of values, including quantifiable elements (e.g., economic value) and characteristics that do not lend themselves as easily to measurement but are nevertheless central (e.g., social and cultural value).

The existing research on live music in cities has identified a range of conditions that affects the quality of live music ecologies. Johansson and Bell (2009) made a helpful overview of factors that influence the formation of local scenes, comprising of the three dimensions of geography, culture, and economy. This includes factors such as relative location of a city, size of place, music industry infrastructure, individual innovators, and migration. Furthermore, researchers have pointed out the importance of a city's infrastructure such as the public transport network (Whiting & Carter, 2016). Next, the "soft infrastructure" matters for the strength of live music ecologies. This includes a strong local network of people and skills, which fits into the "wider socio-spatial fabric of the city" (Brown et al., 2000, p. 445). The soft infrastructure includes the role of gatekeepers in creating strong local music scenes that support inclusivity and creativity (Gallan, 2012) and the role of venue owners who need to navigate conflicting cultural, commercial, and regulatory forces (Carah et al., 2020). Furthermore, music boards and night mayors are understood as key actors to represent the interests of the nightlife sector (Terrill et al., 2015; Webster et al., 2018). They can lobby for favorable policy and regulation, such as non-restrictive licensing conditions that support live music provision at late hours. Finally, live music ecologies can be supported through urban planning, for example by the "agent of change" principle that protects live music venues from noise complaints following from encroaching residential development (Ross, 2017).

Of course, each city has its own "mix" of how these different conditions are met. In a comparison of live music policies in Dutch cities, Hitters and Mulder (2020) observe a strong path dependency, "The provision of live music and festivals of each city and their respective policies can be explained by the history and identity of the city in question" (p. 12). The notion of path dependency is used in evolutionary economic geography to analyze the spatial patterns and dynamics of the emergence and growth of industrial development in particular regions. This concept is thus closely related to ecological thinking (Berg & Hassink, 2014; Martin & Sunley, 2006). It denotes a process where the outcome evolves as a consequence of historical choices, spatial characteristics, existing institutions, and contingencies. Behr et al. (2016) use a similar argument about the ecologies of live music when pointing at "the complexities of relationships across time: while a gig is always necessarily taking place here and now, it is also bound into an ecological development of how gigs happened in the past and how they will happen in the future" (p. 20).

Cities differ in the genres that dominate local scenes and the relative importance of particular festivals or venues. Furthermore, cities tend to have a local understanding of their character that might affect their approaches to cultural production and policymaking. Notwithstanding the importance of such local specifics, it is vital to also recognize how developments on other geographical scales affect urban live music ecologies. Of course, local live music actors have to comply with national laws and policies. Furthermore, within a country there can be competition between cities to host particular festivals, to attract touring acts, or to establish (sponsored) flagship venues (Aalst & van Melik, 2012; Behr et al., 2016; Kronenburg, 2019). This interurban competition can extend to an international level, where global cities seek to be included in the world tours of famous artists (Short et al., 1996). The live music sector is a key example of globalization, with international fan communities and conglomerates (e.g., LiveNation). Even policy approaches are mobile, as "global policy assemblages" (Bennett, 2020; see also Johansson in this volume) such as the music city concept spread internationally through handbooks and "touring consultants" commissioned by cities. This demonstrates that local live music ecologies are embedded in interrelated national and international networks.

As we argue in the next section, the city of Rotterdam is a case in point of how local and international developments coalesce. We contribute to the existing literature by distinguishing four different values of live music, which take shape in the context of the (inter)national music industry. In the next section, we will describe this city, before turning to these values and how they are achieved in Rotterdam.

3   ROTTERDAM'S CULTURAL POLICY AND URBAN DEVELOPMENT

Rotterdam is the second city of the Netherlands, dominated by an enormous port, the largest of Europe. It is a city that is not only closely connected to other cities in the polycentric Randstad area, but also a hub in a European and global network of trade, transport, and logistics (Hall & Pain, 2006). The bustling port city was severely damaged in the Second World War, wiping away most of the city center. In the decades to follow, the city was rebuilt according to a modernist agenda including a new cultural infrastructure of museums, concert halls, and theaters. As Van Ulzen (2007) argues, this era of reconstruction is closely related to the image and identity of Rotterdam as a modern metropolis characterized by a hands-on and down-to-earth mentality.

An international and global orientation was part and parcel of Rotterdam's strategies for urban development. As mentioned above, the international modernist movement in architecture and urban planning inspired the reconstruction of the city. But emerging ideas on the use of culture for urban development also caught on very early in Rotterdam (Bianchini & Parkinson, 1993). An example is the adoption of the creative city concept as a global policy assemblage (Bennett, 2020), inspired by the work of Charles Landry and Franco Bianchini (1995) and Richard Florida (2002). Waterfront and port redevelopments (e.g., the Kop van Zuid) were modeled after successful urban regeneration examples from across the globe, including Baltimore, Barcelona, New York, and Glasgow (Doucet, 2013). International experts and consultants were engaged for research and advisory reports. A recent example is the International Advisory Board's report on culture (IABx Rotterdam, 2017). It firmly established the convergence of cultural policy, urban planning, and economic development policy.

As early as the 1980s, popular music became a focal point in the city's expanding cultural policy. There was public support available for youth centers and venues programming popular music as well as for music festivals. These gradually became part of the subsidized cultural infrastructure of the city (Shapiro, 2020). Like in other Dutch cities, the city government has a strong influence on the live music ecology, as many venues and festivals rely on public support. The local government shapes practices in the ecology through funding guidelines and policy requirements. In Rotterdam, festivals in particular were considered to be excellent vehicles for city marketing while simultaneously allowing for accessible and participatory cultural activities. Large cultural expos aimed at supralocal audiences were already organized every five years in the decades of reconstruction. To coordinate the many events in Rotterdam, a dedicated coordinating organization called "Rotterdam Festivals" was established in 1993 (Shapiro, 2020). With a popular music policy vision plan (City Government of Rotterdam, 2007), popular music matured as a legitimate subject of public support. Core venues were selected, which would receive structural funding from the city, but it also signaled a gap in performance opportunities. In 2019, this policy was strengthened with a new vision document which firmly established pop music as a legitimate field of policy intervention and support for urban development and sustainable growth (City Government of Rotterdam, 2019).

In this city which, according to a popular saying, is never finished, the infrastructure for live music has been the topic of heated public and political debates. The city made several attempts to establish a venue for popular music for 1000 to 2000 people, competing with similar venues in neighboring cities Amsterdam, The Hague, and Utrecht. Such a venue would make Rotterdam a logical stop for international acts touring the European continent (Hitters & Mulder, 2020). Interestingly, the absence of this venue encouraged music professionals in Rotterdam to collaborate, discuss, and share programming opportunities. As Hitters and Mulder explain, this became known as the Rotterdam Model: a network of bookers, event organizers, promoters and programmers, based on trust and collegial cooperation, programming local live music events, using several spaces all over the city which before had never been used for live music.

Rotterdam not only has a strong heritage in, among others, electronic dance music (Van der Hoeven, 2014), but also a vivid contemporary music scene with particular strengths in urban and hip-hop genres. While the infrastructure is generally not perceived as perfect, even with recent additions of Maassilo and RTM stage (see Sect. 4.3), the city has a strong support structure for live music (Van der Ploeg, 2020). Its soft infrastructure consists of a particularly strong network and collegial collaboration, which allows for diverse and complete offerings of live music. These are all indications of the high quality of Rotterdam's live music ecology.

4   Live Music and Urban Development in Rotterdam

As set out in the literature review, we understand Rotterdam's live music ecology as a network of venues, festivals, and social actors that enable live music performances. This ecology is not only shaped by local and historical developments, but also by actors on national and international scales. Within this ecology, four different values (economic, cultural, social, and spatial) are dynamically negotiated by the different actors, such as music professionals, residents, and policymakers. These values follow on from our earlier research, which was based on a qualitative content analysis of live music reports and strategies (Van der Hoeven & Hitters, 2019) and in-depth interviews with policymakers, festival organizers, and venue owners (Van der Hoeven & Hitters, 2020b). Based on these analyses, the concept of spatial value was added to the common tripartite distinction between cultural, social, and economic value (Klamer, 2004). These values concern the specific ways in which stakeholders perceive the benefits of live music for cities and their inhabitants, which we will discuss in turn for the case of Rotterdam.

4.1   Economic Value

Academic discussions about the economic value of culture have been dominated by cultural economics approaches to this issue. Within the field of cultural economics, there is consensus on what the economic value of culture consists of and how this relates to other values, such as cultural or social values (Klamer, 2004; Throsby, 2001). In economics, value refers to the price of goods—what people are willing to pay in exchange for a good or service. Economic value may take different forms and it can be calculated, for instance, as the total sum of revenue that is generated within a given economic sector. The expected economic effects are also powerful justifications for investments in culture. In music, there are ample examples of so-called economic impact studies which calculate the effect of investments in, for instance, a new music venue or a festival (Australasian Performing Right Association, 2011; UK Music, 2016). Value is understood as the economic effects of generated revenue, jobs that are created, and additional spending by visitors and tourists in the local economy. Such economic arguments are quite common in public discussions on the value of music and serve as an effective legitimation of public support and private investments.

Rotterdam is no exception. As indicated above, the city has explicitly dedicated policies toward furthering the music sector, which were always justified using an economic rationale. The clearest example of a focus on economic effects is a report by the now defunct Economic Development Board Rotterdam in 2008. The board was an advisory committee, made up of high ranked public officials and business leaders, aimed at furthering the economic growth agenda of the city. Interestingly, while the Rotterdam Council for Art and Culture—the city's cultural policy advisor—developed its first vision on the significance of popular music (*Rotterdamse Raad voor Kunst en Cultuur*, 2006), the board evidenced the economic value of popular music. It stated:

> [I]t is surprising to us that while the audio-visual sector is viewed as an economic sector, with its own dedicated economic policy, the music industry is not yet recognized as such. Municipal policy and discussions in the city deal almost always with issues of cultural policy, venues, festivals, and sometimes also education. Up until now, however, there is no attention paid to the economic importance of pop music. (Economic Development Board Rotterdam, 2008, p. 7)[1]

The report concludes with a plea for an economic policy aimed at the music industry, or that at least complements cultural policy with a stronger

---

[1] All Dutch quotes translated by the authors.

focus the economic value of music. In addition, it calls for intensification of cooperation within the industry on a local level, between commercial entrepreneurs and (partly) subsidized organizations and venues. This preludes the emergence of the Rotterdam Model of flexible programming.

In a similar vein, festivals are particularly justified based on their economic value, as posited in the opening remarks of a document on event policy:

> Ever more people from outside the city come to Rotterdam. Over half of the visitors to the North Sea Jazz Festival, International Film Festival Rotterdam, Metropolis, World Port Days, and the Summer Carnival come from outside the city. That is good for the city's economy and for employment. These events are especially good for the image of the city. There is probably no other activity where Rotterdam so often and so positively reaches the headlines of the newspapers. (Rotterdam Festivals, 2009. p. 6)

The economic value of live music is an integral part of Rotterdam's policy aimed at furthering cultural provisions. In the most recent policy document, it is clearly acknowledged that (live) music offers opportunities for economic development and adds to the metropolitan image and attractiveness of the city for residents, visitors, and business (City Government of Rotterdam, 2019). The economic values of live music for urban development are crucial for justifying investments in infrastructure and programming. Nevertheless, in this super-diverse and transforming city, economic objectives are complemented with additional values underlying dedicated support for live music. These cultural, social, and spatial values are explored in the next sections.

4.2   Cultural Value

The cultural value of live music in urban development concerns the role of musical creativity, cultural vibrancy, and talent development (Van der Hoeven & Hitters, 2020b). Musical creativity refers to the intrinsic value of live music and how it acts as a source of inspiration and artistic development. It is at the heart of all the other values, as the diverse effects of live music ultimately follow from musical creativity. For example, cities are often known for particular musical developments that can become part of their identity and urban branding (Wissmann, 2014). In Rotterdam, this is the case for its contributions to dance music in the 1990s and hip-hop in the past decades. The next dimension of cultural vibrancy reflects live music's contribution to the wider cultural sector in a city. A vibrant live music ecology includes a range of different genres and scenes, which add to the general cultural offerings of a city. Finally, the dimension of talent development concerns the ways in which cities provide opportunities for people to hone their skills. This matters not just for emerging performers, who need stages of varying sizes to gradually build up their career, but also for ancillary jobs in the live music sector (e.g., technicians or marketers). In that way, talent development can be considered an essential precondition to enhance musical creativity and cultural vibrancy.

The central goals of Rotterdam's current cultural policies are strongly focused on providing the right conditions for talent to develop: "The Board of Mayor and Aldermen seeks to support and enable (new) cultural makers to professionalize, to organize, to develop and to present themselves, in the conviction that we thereby contribute to a sustainable cultural climate," according to the City Government of Rotterdam (2019, p. 4). The city's popular music policy specifies how popular music adds to these goals: "A strong popular music sector provides a broad range of cultural offerings for a diverse audience, so desired by the city, and it allows talents to excel" (Ibid.). These statements need to be understood against the background of various challenges to talent development in Rotterdam. A vital issue is the perceived lack of affordable spaces to rehearse and perform, which is a consequence of the growing popularity of Rotterdam and rising rents. Another challenge to talent development is the labor market position of artists, as musicians struggle to generate a sustainable income from their profession (Van der Hoeven & Hitters, 2020a; Webster et al., 2018).

These challenges are of course not exclusive to Rotterdam. Many researchers have observed in other countries how gentrification poses significant challenges to small-scale cultural production and affordable housing for creative people (Cohen, 2013; Lobato, 2006). Live music can play a vital role in urban development, but the gentrifying city, in turn, is not necessarily conducive to musical creativity, cultural vibrancy, and talent development. Furthermore, it has been noted in the literature how wider inequalities in society are reflected in the "superstar economy" of the (live) music industry. A small segment of highly successful performers earns a very large part of the revenues (Krueger, 2019). Arguably, this is one of the key reasons why the ecology concept is widely adopted in both academic and policy circles. This concept underscores the importance of diversity in providing performance opportunities for musicians in different phases of their career (Behr et al., 2016). A healthy live music ecology is vital for artistic development and securing the talent pipeline for the future.

4.3   Social Value

Live music is a vital element in the social life of cities. For example, people meet at concerts, migrant communities find shared spaces for musical activities, and live shows are places where fan identities are affirmed (Sánchez-Fuarros, 2013; Van der Hoeven & Hitters, 2019). The social value of live music concerns different ways in which relationships between people are sustained. It consists of the dimensions of social capital, public engagement, and identity (Van der Hoeven & Hitters, 2019). The first dimension of social capital explains how live music enhances a sense of belonging within specific communities (i.e., bonding social capital) and allows connections between people with different backgrounds (i.e., bridging social capital). As we have argued elsewhere:

> Live music ecologies that support the social capital of urban communities function as spaces where different groups of people can develop social networks and meet each other. This implies that they support live music participation for all ages, genders, and communities. (Van der Hoeven & Hitters, 2019, p. 266)

The second dimension of public engagement concerns the activities of live music organizations to make a positive impact on cities and their inhabitants. Many festivals and venues are not just focused on music, but they want to contribute to other local goals. For example, they might engage in fundraising, provide a space for community organizations, organize social activities for people in the neighborhood, or support political causes. Finally, the dimension of identity reflects the role of live music in attachment to place. People can derive a sense of identity and cultural pride from local cultural accomplishments. For example, festivals and venues are often places where identities are sustained and become landmarks that people identify with.

Such feelings of identity and cultural pride are prominent in Rotterdam. Similar to other second cities, Rotterdam is very well aware of its identity in relation to that of Amsterdam. This involves a strong sense of pride. Even in the report discussing the city's popular music policy, this is apparent: "We are unambiguous in our ambition: we do not attempt to be a second Amsterdam or Utrecht, we do things 'Rotterdam style'" (City Government of Rotterdam, 2019, p. 24). This statement is a response to the perceived lack of a dedicated popular music venue in Rotterdam, as discussed in Sect. 3. Compared to Amsterdam and Utrecht, the Rotterdam Model is more focused on festivals and booking bands in a range of different spaces that are not necessarily dedicated to just live music (e.g., clubs and restaurants) (Hitters & Mulder, 2020). Repeatedly, the policy report boasts the accomplishments the city can be proud of, such as successful artists from the region, the strong presence of youth cultures, and the diversity of popular music stages.

These achievements notwithstanding, Rotterdam faces many social challenges that have an impact on the city's cultural policies as well. In particular, the urban areas south of the river Maas struggle with social inequality, poverty, and crime. The socio-spatial inequalities in the city are reflected in cultural provision:

> In terms of the location of cultural supply, we observe a concentration of venues and festivals in the northern part of Rotterdam. We see opportunities for audience growth and to broaden the audience in Rotterdam South. (City Government of Rotterdam, 2019, p. 25)

To address the major socio-cultural challenges in Rotterdam South, a national program was launched in 2011, involving a wide range of stakeholders such as the municipality, schools, healthcare organizations, and the police. Culture was added as a new pillar in the program's activities for the period 2019–2022, aiming to enhance the cultural provision and facilities for talent development in Rotterdam South (*Nationaal Programma Rotterdam Zuid*, 2019). The role of culture in personal development is recognized as a vital element to realize the other social and educational goals of the program. Furthermore, the program explores the opportunities for an iconic cultural institution in this part of the city. With references to international examples, such as city museum the MAS in Antwerp and the Elbphilharmonie concert hall in Hamburg, the report argues that a new building can be a driver of tourism and urban development in Rotterdam South. As part of this program, the city government and various cultural and educational institutions are currently planning a "culture campus." Furthermore, the city government expressed the wish that the new multifunctional theater (*Theater Zuidplein*), which opened in 2020, will also be used for programming popular music (City Government of Rotterdam, 2019). In the same year during the global pandemic, the RTM Stage was opened. This is a new venue for 7800 visitors in Rotterdam's convention center and multi-purpose arena, located in the same area as the theater. In the coming post-Covid years, these venues have to prove their contribution to a more inclusive live music ecology that extends to the southern part of the city. This example of the National Programme Rotterdam South underscores how social, spatial, economic, and cultural issues are interrelated.

Of course, similar issues of inclusivity are faced by other cities to varying degrees. It is widely established in popular music research that patterns of popular music production and consumption are affected by socio-economic, ethnic, and gender divisions (e.g., Grazian, 2009; Schaap, 2019; Strong & Raine, 2019; Willekens & Daenekindt, 2020). Examples of these issues are a lack of cultural facilities for lower socio-economic strata and a lack of diversity in cultural institutions. A key policy objective in the Netherlands is to make the subsidized activities of cultural organizations more accessible to a wider demographic. To support live music's social value in Rotterdam and beyond, it is vital to enhance inclusivity in live music ecologies and policies.

4.4   Spatial Value

In relation to the other three values, spatial value puts the emphasis on the relationship between live music and the built environment. It focuses on the physical setting of concerts, which both affects and is affected by live music. Live music can have an impact on the urban environment, but at the same time, the spaces where music is performed have an influence on this musical experience. Spatial value consists of the dimensions of performing, (re)developing, and narrating urban space (Van der Hoeven & Hitters, 2020b), which shed light on how live music's relationship to the built environment is shaped. Performing is about the ways in which a city is physically used to stage concerts, redeveloping refers to the role of live music in the regeneration of space, and narrating focuses on live music as part of the stories told about cities (e.g., media, urban branding, and heritage narratives).

The Katendrecht neighborhood in Rotterdam provides a good example of these dimensions. Katendrecht is a peninsula where Rotterdam's red-light district was located. It struggled for many years with high levels of crime, poverty, and a poor reputation. Arguably, Katendrecht is a textbook case of how gentrification transforms neighborhoods in post-industrial cities. The first dimension of spatial value (performing) is apparent in how Katendrecht has provided a rich setting for concerts throughout the years. Even during the Second World War jazz acts continued to perform there. During the occupation, the German authorities did not permit soldiers to go to Katendrecht due to its red-light district (Van der Horst, 2017). As a consequence, some venues in Katendrecht remained open for some time, as the occupying forces were less present here. Spatial value's second dimension of (re)developing is illustrated by the Nacht van de Kaap (i.e., "Night of the Cape") festival, which was organized for the first time in 2008. The festival coincided with a broader communication campaign to improve the neighborhood's reputation entitled "Can you handle the Cape?" Instead of denying Katendrecht's bad reputation, both the festival and the urban branding campaign explicitly adopted a narrative referring to the area's rough history of prostitution and sailor bars to present it as an edgy destination for up-market visitors and residents (see, e.g., the Conversation-Next, 2014, video). During one of the festivals, visitors could acquire promotional information about the residences to be developed in the festival area (Heijmans, 2019). Underscoring the successful transformation, the festival moved to a new location after several editions, because the empty warehouses used for performances were being repurposed to apartments and a museum, as can be seen in Fig. 2.1 (Onnink, 2019). Finally, an example of the spatial value of narrating urban spaces is the ways in which the festival and other historical performances are part of the stories told about Katendrecht in media reports, urban branding, and tourist brochures. In fact, the place where jazz acts performed during the Second World War is now a culture center, which focuses on the heritage of Katendrecht and its inhabitants through storytelling activities (Boonstra & Specht, 2016).

The Katendrecht case illustrates a wider trend toward densification in Rotterdam and the Netherlands in general. Due to housing shortage and the popularity of inner-city living, many new residences are being developed. This process of densification poses new challenges to festivals and live music festivals, such as noise complaints from new neighbors and rising rents following gentrification (Van der Hoeven & Hitters, 2020a). Indeed, the spatial embedding of live music is a key issue in Rotterdam. In the context of densification and gentrification, it is a challenge to keep affordable spaces for creatives to live, rehearse, and perform. This is

Fig. 2.1 These former warehouses were used for a festival that contributed to Katendrecht's placemaking. Meanwhile, one of the warehouses has been redeveloped to residences and shops, while the other is transformed to a Museum of Migration. (Photo credit: Joris, Wikimedia Commons, CC BY-SA 4.0)

underscored by the following quote from Rotterdam's popular music policy: "This city used to have sufficient affordable spaces for artists and other creative individuals. However, the development of Rotterdam and its growing popularity has an impact on the real estate market" (City Government of Rotterdam, 2019, p. 17).

Festivalization is also a challenge to embedding live music in the city. Even though festivals are widely supported in Rotterdam by the local government and citizens alike, their negative impact on the environment has received quite some attention in recent years (Hitters & Mulder, 2020; Van der Hoeven & Hitters, 2020a). This included debates about the unavailability of public parks because of the growing number of commercial festivals and the negative impact on flora (Venema, 2019). This forces the local government and the coordinating agency Rotterdam Festivals to search for new locations to host large-scale events. In the recently adopted spatial strategy (City Government of Rotterdam, 2021), the city government states it wants to strike a better balance between tranquility and a lively city. In 2022, the zoning plans were updated with new regulations on where events are allowed, the maximum number of events and sound levels. On the one hand, this restricts the number of festivals in some places and makes it difficult for new festivals to find a suitable location. On the other hand, the new rules protect the interests of organizers because for new residences close to event locations (i.e., built after the zoning plans were introduced) higher sound levels are accepted (City Government of Rotterdam, n.d.). These new zoning plans led to much debate both before and after the implementation, which underscores the growing complexity of finding space for culture in the changing city.

5   Discussion and Conclusions

In this chapter, we explored the values that are involved in the process of adopting live music for urban development. We did so with a focus on one case, the city of Rotterdam in the Netherlands. The economic, cultural, social, and spatial value of live music feature prominently in debates, policy discourses, and popular discussions in the city. These values represent the different benefits that live music may have for, among other things, the city's image, identity, and development and the wellbeing of its inhabitants. Our analysis of these values enabled us to understand how the various actors in this city seek to manage the impact of live music. Furthermore, it clarifies how the diverse actors in live music ecologies give meaning to this cultural form and the challenges they encounter in achieving the values. Of course, values can also be highly contested and mutually competitive. When economic effects are sought, the social value of a grassroots stage as a community meeting place may suffer. And spatial value may be contested among residents who fear noise and nuisance and a property developer who sees opportunities of using a music venue for revitalizing a neighborhood.

Our analysis shows how value is generated and captured within the context of path dependency and developments on different geographical scales. The specific historical events that have left their marks on the city of Rotterdam have strongly impacted the subsequent choices that were made in urban policy and planning. It has likewise shaped the cultural and musical identity of the city. With respect to the use of live music for urban development, path dependency dates back to the early attempts in the post-Second World War era to use festivals for the redevelopment of urban culture and revitalization of metropolitan identity. Important to note is how, from the onset, the interplay of cultural, economic, social, and spatial value has become entrenched in the city's development policies.

Interestingly, the city has actively participated in and contributed to the global policy assemblages on culture in urban regeneration, the creative city, and music cities.

The latter also signifies how policies aimed at furthering live music for urban development are embedded in the national and international contexts of actors, policies, markets, and the transformation thereof. The values of urban live music ecologies are shaped by the interplay of these geographical levels. In the case of Rotterdam, the city's local live music ecology has a particularly strong soft infrastructure of networks of cooperation and trust. The "Rotterdam model" is a clear example of how soft infrastructure can fill the perceived gaps in the hard infrastructure of brick-and-mortar venues. We would argue that this practice of flexible programming in different venues, enabled by a high level of collaboration within a network of event organizers, programmers, and bookers, has even further strengthened the live music ecology. However, the strong relationships between the local government, venues, and festivals can also pose a risk to the sustainability of Rotterdam's live music ecology, as the reliance on government funding makes live music organizations vulnerable to top-down policy changes and budget cuts.

Of course, the sustainability of a live music ecology is not only dependent on local policies and contexts, but needs to be understood in relation to issues of interurban competition, national geographical structures, and international market developments. Within the polycentric Randstad area, the relative proximity of other urban/metropolitan centers impacts the provision of and demand for live music, as well as the spatial needs for performance places. Real estate markets are influenced by national developments and policies. The globally operating music industries strongly influence the local opportunities for programming live music. For example, touring schedules of international popular music acts limit options for programming headliners for local festivals and stages. This in turn, increases competition on a national and international level.

The relationship between factors on different geographical scales and socio-cultural developments implies that live music ecologies are dynamic. Urban planning and policymaking for live music needs to adapt to this ever-changing context. Indeed, musical creativity cannot be planned in a top-down manner, but it is possible to create conditions for music scenes to thrive. For example, a live music ecology that supports talent development requires sufficient rehearsal spaces and venues of different sizes so that musicians can progressively build up their audience (Behr et al.,

2016). Furthermore, a strong live music ecology supports grassroots creativity and entrepreneurship, involving both informal and formal cultural organizations (Cohendet et al., 2009). As each live music ecology has a different set of values and policy developments, it is impossible to replicate the policies from Rotterdam elsewhere. However, based on our case study we can draw various suggestions for further research in other cities.

The dynamic interplay of geographical levels and the local experiences of the values of live music need to be scrutinized in future academic research. A critical approach to values is key to these endeavors. Too often, the values of live music are traded off against competing fields of policy attention, or values are instrumentalized for broader—often financial—policy goals. In that process, inequalities may be reinforced and injustices may be reproduced. The issue of gentrification and displacement is one of the areas that need to be further investigated, preferably in a comparative manner. Other subjects in need of further attention are the precarious labor conditions of musicians (see Zendel in this volume), professionalization of the live music sector, and issues of sustainability and environmental impact for venues and festivals.

Acknowledgment This work was supported by the Dutch Research Council (NWO) and the Taskforce for Applied Research (NRPO-SIA), grant number 314-99-202, research program Smart Culture—Arts and Culture, as part of the project Staging Popular Music: Researching Sustainable Live Music Ecologies for Artists, Music Venues and Cities (POPLIVE). Partners in this project are Mojo Concerts and The Association of Dutch Pop Music Venues and Festivals (VNPF).

REFERENCES

Aalst, I. V., & van Melik, R. (2012). City festivals and urban development: Does place matter? *European Urban and Regional Studies, 19*(2), 195–206.

Australasian Performing Right Association. (2011). *Economic contribution of the venue-based live music industry in Australia.* APRA.

Ballico, C., & Watson, A. (2020). *Music cities: Evaluating a global cultural policy concept.* Palgrave Macmillan.

Behr, A., Brennan, M., Cloonan, M., Frith, S., & Webster, E. (2016). Live concert performance: An ecological approach. *Rock Music Studies, 3*(1), 5–23.

Bennett, T. (2020). The justification of a music city: Handbooks, intermediaries and value disputes in a global policy assemblage. *City, Culture and Society, 22,* 1–8. https://doi.org/10.1016/j.ccs.2020.100354

Berg, S. H., & Hassink, R. (2014). Creative industries from an evolutionary perspective: A critical literature review. *Geography Compass, 8*(9), 653–664.

Bianchini, F., & Parkinson, M. (Eds.). (1993). *Cultural policy and urban regeneration: The West European experience.* Manchester University Press.

Boonstra, B., & Specht, M. (2016). The appropriated city. In G. De Roo & L. Boelens (Eds.), *Spatial planning in a complex unpredictable world of change* (pp. 122–150). In Planning.

Brown, A., O'Connor, J., & Cohen, S. (2000). Local music policies within a global music industry: Cultural quarters in Manchester and Sheffield. *Geoforum, 31*(4), 437–451.

Carah, N., Regan, S., Goold, L., Rangiah, L., Miller, P., & Ferris, J. (2020). Original live music venues in hyper-commercialised nightlife precincts: Exploring how venue owners and managers navigate cultural, commercial and regulatory forces. *International Journal of Cultural Policy, 27*(2), 1–15. https://doi.org/10.1080/10286632.2020.1830979

City Government of Rotterdam. (2007). *De Visie Op De Lokale Popsector.* [Policy Vision]. Gemeente Rotterdam. Retrieved January 26, 2021, from https://rotterdam.raadsinformatie.nl/document/249502/1#search=%22lokale%20popsector

City Government of Rotterdam. (2019). *Beleidsvisie Pop 2019–2030.* [Policy Vision]. Gemeente Rotterdam. Retrieved January 26, 2021, from https://rotterdam.notubiz.nl/document/7569447/1

City Government of Rotterdam. (2021). *De Veranderstad—Werken aan een wereldstad voor iedereen. Omgevingsvisie Rotterdam* [City of change—Working on a global city for everyone. Spatial strategy Rotterdam]. Gemeente Rotterdam.

City Government of Rotterdam. (n.d.). *Parapluherziening evenementen: Regels.* Retrieved August 27, 2022, from https://www.ruimtelijkeplannen.nl/documents/NL.IMRO.0599.BP1137PapluEvemnt-va01/r_NL.IMRO.0599.BP1137PapluEvemnt-va01.html

Cohen, S. (2012). Live music and urban landscape: Mapping the beat in Liverpool. *Social Semiotics, 22*(5), 587–603.

Cohen, S. (2013). "From the big dig to the big gig": Live music, urban regeneration and social change in the European Capital of Culture 2008. In C. Wergin & F. Holt (Eds.), *Musical performance and the changing city: Post-industrial contexts in Europe and the United States* (pp. 27–51). Routledge.

Cohendet, P., Grandadam, D., & Simon, L. (2009). Economics and the ecology of creativity: Evidence from the popular music industry. *International Review of Applied Economics, 23*(6), 709–722.

Conversation-next. (2014). *Can you handle the cape?* [Video]. Retrieved January 21, 2021, from https://vimeo.com/102607856

Doucet, B. (2013). Variations of the entrepreneurial city: Goals, roles and visions in Rotterdam's Kop van Zuid and the Glasgow Harbour Megaprojects. *International Journal of Urban and Regional Research, 37*(6), 2035–2051.

Economic Development Board Rotterdam. (2008). *A little less conversation. (A little more action please). Over de economische potentie van de muziekindustrie in Rotterdam.* [Advisory report]. Economic Development Board Rotterdam. Retrieved January 27, 2021, from https://www.esseboom.net/wp-content/uploads/2014/11/A-little-less-conversation-2008.pdf

Florida, R. (2002). *The rise of the creative class.* Basic Books.

Gallan, B. (2012). Gatekeeping night spaces: The role of booking agents in creating 'local' live music venues and scenes. *Australian Geographer, 43*(1), 35–50.

Grazian, D. (2009). Urban nightlife, social capital, and the public life of cities. *Sociological Forum, 24*(4), 908–917.

Hall, P. G., & Pain, K. (2006). *The polycentric metropolis: Learning from mega-city regions in Europe.* Routledge.

Heijmans. (2019). *Fenix 1. Katendrecht Rotterdam.* Retrieved January 21, 2021, from https://issuu.com/conversation-next/docs/boek_fenix_i_katendrecht_nov2019

Hitters, E., & Mulder, M. (2020). Live music ecologies and festivalisation: The role of urban live music policies. *International Journal of Music Business Research, 9*(2), 38–57.

Holt, F. (2010). The economy of live music in the digital age. *European Journal of Cultural Studies, 13*(2), 243–261.

IABx Rotterdam [International Advisory Board Expert Edition]. (2017). *Rotterdam, stay close to what you are! Becoming an international cultural hotspot, starts with authenticity.* Gemeente Rotterdam. Retrieved January 27, 2021, from https://en.rotterdampartners.nl/app/uploads//2019/03/IABx-2017-On-Culture-report.pdf

Johansson, O., & Bell, T. L. (2009). Where are the new US music scenes? In O. Johansson & T. L. Bell (Eds.), *Sound, society, and the geography of popular music* (pp. 219–239). Ashgate.

Klamer, A. (2004). Cultural goods are good for more than their economic value. In V. Rao & M. Walton (Eds.), *Culture and public action* (pp. 138–162). The International Bank for Reconstruction and Development/The World Bank. Stanford University Press.

Kronenburg, R. (2019). *This must be the place: An architectural history of popular music performance venues.* Bloomsbury Academic.

Kronenburg, R. (2020). Sound spaces. Pop music concerts and festivals in urban environments. In E. Mazierska, L. Gillon, & T. Rigg (Eds.), *The future of live music* (pp. 131–149). Bloomsbury.

Krueger, A. B. (2019). *Rockonomics: A backstage tour of what the music industry can teach us about economics and life.* Currency.

Landry, C., & Bianchini, F. (1995). *The creative city*. Demos/Comedia.

Lobato, R. (2006). Gentrification, cultural policy and live music in Melbourne. *Media International Australia, 120*, 63–75.

Martin, R., & Sunley, P. (2006). Path dependence and regional economic evolution. *Journal of Economic Geography, 6*(4), 395–437.

Mulder, M., Hitters, E., & Rutten, P. (2020). The impact of festivalization on the Dutch live music action field: A thematic analysis. *Creative Industries Journal, 1–24*. https://doi.org/10.1080/17510694.2020.1815396

Nationaal Programma Rotterdam Zuid [National Program Rotterdam South]. (2019). *Uitvoeringsplan 2019–2022*. Retrieved January 20, 2021, from www.nprz.nl/over-nprz/onze-documenten/uitvoeringsplan

Onnink, G. (2019, February 1). Verhuizing naar ss Rotterdam 'geschenk uit de hemel' voor Nacht van de Kaap. *Algemeen Dagblad*. Retrieved January 28, 2021, from https://www.ad.nl/rotterdam/verhuizing-naar-ss-rotterdam-geschenk-uit-de-hemel-voor-nacht-van-de-kaap~a89af6b0/

Ross, S. (2017). Protecting urban spaces of intangible cultural heritage and nightlife community subcultural wealth: International and national strategies, the agent of change, principle, and creative placekeeping. *Western Journal of Legal Studies, 7*(1), 1–20.

Rotterdam Festivals. (2009). *Dieper in de stad, verder in de wereld. Aanscherping Evenementenbeleid*. Rotterdam Festivals.

Rotterdamse Raad voor kunst en Cultuur [The Rotterdam Council for Art and Culture]. (2006). *Rotterdam has got that pop*. Retrieved January 27, 2021, from https://www.rrkc.nl/wp-content/uploads/2006/01/rotterdam-has-got-that-pop-incl-cover.pdf

Sánchez-Fuarros, I. (2013). Sounding out the Cuban diaspora in Barcelona: Music, migration and the urban experience. In F. Holt & C. Wergin (Eds.), *Musical performance and the changing city post-industrial contexts in Europe and the United States* (pp. 77–101). Routledge.

Schaap, J. (2019). *Elvis has finally left the building? Boundary work, whiteness and the reception of rock music in comparative perspective*. Doctoral dissertation, Erasmus University Rotterdam.

Scholten, P., Crul, M., & Van de Laar, P. T. (2019). *Coming to terms with superdiversity: The case of Rotterdam*. Springer.

Shapiro, E. (2020). *Small venues as networking nodes. Live music in the context of creative city development*. Thesis, MA Global Markets, Local Creativities, Erasmus University Rotterdam.

Short, J. R., Kim, Y., Kuus, M., & Wells, H. (1996). The dirty little secret of world cities research: Data problems in comparative analysis. *International Journal of Urban and Regional Research, 20*(4), 697–717.

Strong, C., & Raine, S. (2019). *Towards gender equality in the music industry: Education, practice and strategies for change*. Bloomsbury Academic.

Swartjes, B., & Berkers, P. (2022). How music festival organisers in Rotterdam deal with diversity. In A. Smith, G. Osborn, & B. Quinn (Eds.), *Festivals and the city: The contested geographies of urban events* (pp. 95–109). University of Westminster Press.

Terrill, A., Hogarth, D., Clement, A., & Francis, R. (2015). *Mastering of a music city.* http://www.ifpi.org/downloads/The-Mastering-of-a-Music-City.pdf

Throsby, C. D. (2001). *Economics and culture.* Cambridge University Press.

UK Music. (2016). *Wish You Were Here 2016. The contribution of live music to the UK economy.* UK Music.

Van der Hoeven, A. (2014). Remembering the popular music of the 1990s: Dance music and the cultural meanings of decade-based nostalgia. *International Journal of Heritage Studies, 20*(3), 316–330.

Van der Hoeven, A., & Hitters, E. (2019). The social and cultural values of live music: Sustaining urban live music ecologies. *Cities, 90,* 263–271.

Van der Hoeven, A., & Hitters, E. (2020a). Challenges for the future of live music: A review of contemporary developments in the live music sector. In E. Mazierska, L. Gillon, & T. Rigg (Eds.), *The future of live music* (pp. 34–50). Bloomsbury.

Van der Hoeven, A., & Hitters, E. (2020b). The spatial value of live music: Performing, (re)developing and narrating urban spaces. *Geoforum, 117,* 154–164.

Van der Hoeven, A., Hitters, E., Berkers, P., Mulder, M., & Everts, R. (2020). Theorising the production and consumption of live music: A critical review. In E. Mazierska, L. Gillon, & T. Rigg (Eds.), *The future of live music* (pp. 19–33). Bloomsbury.

Van der Horst, H. (2017). *Rotterdam: Bruid van de Maas.* Prometheus.

Van der Ploeg, P. (2020, December 11). Met het 'RTM Stage' heeft Rotterdam er een grote, flexibele popzaal bij. *NRC Handelsblad.* Retrieved January 28, 2021, from https://www.nrc.nl/nieuws/2020/12/11/met-het-rtm-stage-heeft-rotterdam-er-een-grote-flexibele-popzaal-bij-a4023550

Van Ulzen, P. (2007). *Imagine a metropolis: Rotterdam's creative class, 1970–2000.* 010 Publishers.

Venema, A. (2019, November 21). Festivals op meer plekken in stad om parken en buren vaker rust te geven. *Algemeen Dagblad.* Retrieved January 28, 2021, from https://www.ad.nl/rotterdam/festivals-op-meer-plekken-in-stad-om-parken-en-buren-vaker-rust-te-geven~ad3dc9ad/

Webster, E., Brennan, M., Behr, A., Cloonan, M., & Ansel, J. (2018). *Valuing live music: The UK live music census 2017 report.* University of Edinburgh/Live Music Exchange.

Whiting, S., & Carter, D. (2016). Access, place and Australian live music. *M/C Journal, 19*(3). http://journal.media-culture.org.au/index.php/mcjournal/article/view/1085

Willekens, M., & Daenekindt, S. (2020). Cultural logics and modes of consumption: Unraveling the multiplicity of symbolic distinctions among concert audiences. *Musicae Scientiae, 26*(1), 24–45. https://doi.org/10.1177/1029864920908305

Wissmann, T. (2014). *Geographies of urban sound*. Ashgate.

CHAPTER 3

The Music Cities Movement and Circulation of Best Practices: A North American Case Study

Ola Johansson

Abstract Cities across the United States and elsewhere want a thriving music ecosystem. The reasons are multifold; the music industry plays a role in the local economy, music is an important community-enhancing activity, and creative activities such as music-making contribute to desirably exciting and cosmopolitan places. These objectives have spurred a music cities movement where previous fragmented policies toward local music are increasingly replaced by a comprehensive approach among urban stakeholders. How and where do new ideas about music and cities take shape and circulate? One such "microspace" is the Music Policy Forum where non-profits, city officials, the music industry, and others share best practices. As an attendee of the 2019 Music Policy Forum in Washington DC, I conducted an analysis of the presentations, panels, and informal discussions that took place there. This participant observation

O. Johansson (✉)
University of Pittsburgh at Johnstown, Johnstown, PA, USA
e-mail: johans@pitt.edu

O. Johansson et al. (eds.), *New Geographies of Music 1*, Geographies
of Media, https://doi.org/10.1007/978-981-99-0757-1_3

revealed a series of music and urban/economic/community development discourses that focused on organizational structures, strategy formation, funding opportunities and limitations, and on-the-ground challenges in the urban landscape. Multiple point and counterpoints offered by the participants suggest that best practices must be sensitive to local circumstances.

Keywords Music policy • Music cities • Participant observation • Discourse analysis • Policy mobilities • Music ecosystem

1   Introduction

The term "music cities" is increasingly common. Media portray some places as having the reputation and characteristics that makes them music cities. The criteria range from cities' attraction as music tourism destinations, their influence on music history, or being the best places for artists to live and work. Most importantly, music cities have an abundance of music venues and a thriving music scene. Beyond the large music industry centers of New York, London, and Los Angeles, American cities such as Nashville, Seattle, Austin, and New Orleans are frequently mentioned. For example, in a series of articles in *CityLab* (e.g., Gardner, 2017; Capps, 2019; Small, 2019) music is considered an important element in urban place-making; therefore, local policy-makers and other stakeholders have joined a budding global music cities movement.

Some cities have a long-standing association with music. For example, Nashville is known as "Music City USA" and Austin as "The Live Music Capital of the World" (Baker, 2016; Hill, 2016; Wynn, 2015). Other cities have also engaged in small-scale, ad hoc music projects that are meant to enhance imageability and/or advance economic development (e.g., Seman, 2010). However, the comprehensive integration of music strategies into local policy-making among a broader set of cities, as evident later in this chapter, is a relatively new phenomenon. Academic research on the subject is therefore also in an emerging state (Baker, 2019; Ballico & Watson, 2020). The objective of this chapter is to investigate the formation and circulation of ideas, beliefs, and objectives that influence music city policies. How and where do new ideas take shape and circulate? The number of "experts" in the field is quite small. They may live and work in different cities but many are connected to and influence each other. The Music Policy Forum (MPF) is one event where non-profits, city officials, the music industry, academics, and others share best practices. As an attendee of the MPF held in October 2019, at Georgetown University in Washington DC, I conducted a discourse analysis of the presentations, panels, and informal discussions that took place there, using the ethnographic method of embedded participant observation. The event attracted almost exclusively participants from North America and, therefore, the discussion focused on issues that are relevant in a North American context, although the concept of music cities is global in scope.

2   Literature Review

The Literature Review consists of two parts. First, the idea of music cities is explored and how it relates to other similar concepts. Then, in order to understand how and where knowledge about music cities takes shape and circulate, the concept of policy mobilities is discussed.

2.1   What Is a Music City?

Increasingly, urban policy has recognized that music can make a vital contribution to both the economy and culture of cities. Therefore, music cities as a component of cultural policy, adopted around the world, needs to be further assessed (Ballico & Watson, 2020). The dominant narrative has been within the realm of political economy discourses, but music cities also have "social, cultural and emotional value" (Baker, 2019, p. 301). The creation of music cities is, on the one hand, an outcome of complex path-dependent historical local processes, but on the other hand also a product of discursive myth-making and urban marketing (Sánchez Fuarros, 2017). It is in this intersection that city governments coordinate music city strategies. In the past, efforts were mostly piecemeal, but increasingly, there is a comprehensive music cities policy approach, often involving formal plans and policies. An early formal music city recognition is UNESCO's "City of Music" program, which was launched in 2006. To receive this designation, cities have to be broadly recognized as center of music with festivals and events, a music industry, music education, and spaces for music production and consumption (UNESCO, 2021).

A key document for the music cities movement was the 2015 global report *The Mastering of a Music City*, produced by the International Federation of the Phonographic Industry (IFPI) and a national non-profit trade organization, Music Canada. The report states that, "a Music City, by its simplest definition, is a place with a vibrant music economy. There is growing recognition among governments and other stakeholders that Music Cities can deliver significant economic, employment, cultural and social benefits" (Terrill et al., 2015, p. 5). Furthermore, it points out that

> the term 'Music City' is becoming widely used in cultural communities and has penetrated the political vernacular in many cities around the world. Once identified solely with Tennessee's storied capital of songwriting and music business, Nashville, Music City now also describes communities of various sizes that have a vibrant music economy which they actively promote. (p. 10)

Intended as a "roadmap" for cities around the world, the report identifies seven key music strategies emphasizing bureaucratic and policy structures, communication, and music infrastructure development (Table 3.1).

The underlying objective of music cities is the creation, expansion, and maintenance of a music *ecosystem*. The term ecosystem is apropos here as alternative concepts are too narrow in scope. Some cities are centers of the *music industry* which consists of companies that produce, publish, market, and sell recorded music and, increasingly, live music (Wikström, 2019). The concept of *scenes* places the artistic and creative side of music at the center (see Bennett & Peterson, 2004; Connell & Gibson, 2003; Kruse, 2010; Straw, 1991). The concept is multifaceted but implies a local style of music, interconnectedness among artists, and musical creativity and innovation. The music ecosystem concept, though, bridges the dichotomy

Table 3.1 Key music city strategies (based on Terrill et al. (2015))

---
1. Music-friendly and musician-friendly policies
2. A music office or officer
3. A music advisory board
4. Engaging the broader music community to get their buy-in and support
5. Access to spaces and places (e.g., venues and rehearsal spaces)
6. Audience development
7. Music tourism

---

of music industry and scenes, as well as incorporating people, entities, and structures often excluded from how music industry and scenes are usually conceptualized. Schippers (2015) defines a music ecosystem as a

> whole system—not only a specific music genre, but the entire complex—of factors defining the genesis, development and sustainability of the surrounding music culture in the widest sense, including the role of individuals, communities, values and attitudes, learning processes, contexts for making music, infrastructure and organizations, rights and regulations, diaspora and travel, media and the music industry. (p. 137)

Baker (2017) suggests that there are three dimensions of a local music ecosystem (Table 3.2). The first dimension is economic and can be measured by variables such as revenue, employment, and the number of venues. The second dimension is creativity—cities need spaces and infrastructure to encourage creative endeavors. Moreover, creative activities are attracted to (and reinforce) cities that are perceived as exciting and cosmopolitan (Florida, 2014). The amount of creative local talent is crucial for creating music cities. The third theme is heritage—cities that are known for a particular genre of music as part of their "cultural DNA." This can be reinforced, and even created, by mechanisms such as music education, community-building activities, and reputation-enhancing events.

The literature has also identified a set of challenges for music city strategies. Ross (2017b) finds a disconnect between plan and reality and governance systems which do not effectively engage with grassroots groups. Grodach (2013) also unveil problems where different interests and

Table 3.2 Dimensions and variables of music city ecosystems (based on Baker (2017))

Economic dimension	Creative dimension	Heritage dimension
All genres of music[a]	Technology	Music heritage
Financial impact	Tolerance	Music-making (live, recorded, production)
Employment figures	Talent	Music education
Audience participation	Territorial assets[b]	Community involvement
Live music venues		Local music events
		International music events

[a] Baker suggests that most economic analyses only focus on one genre of music
[b] Referring to the general livability s of a city

government agencies use creative city discourses for their own goals and agendas, resulting in fragmented strategies.

The capitalist imperative of urban redevelopment also conflicts with music city objectives. Older music venues and other urban spaces, as part of a local music ecosystem, are heritage assets that can enhance a city's vibrancy and reputation as a music city but tends to be undervalued compared to urban redevelopment projects, such as upscale apartments and mixed-use complexes. The "city's development initiatives risk counterproductively destroying the precise characteristics they are otherwise seeking to nourish, create, and, even, commodify" (Ross, 2017a, pp. 32–33). Especially the spaces of live music are subject to gentrification which leads to rising rents, noise complaints, and the much debated problem of "venue death" (Urban Land Institute, 2016; Pollock, 2015). There are different spatial strategies of how to address regulations of music venues. For example, venues can be protected from noise complaints and incompatible developments in designated "entertainment precincts" (Burke & Schmidt, 2013).

2.2   *Policy Mobilities*

To understand how music policy circulates, this section draws from the policy mobilities literature, which is primarily associated with geographer Eugene McCann and his research collaborators. In essence, policy mobilities focus on the social processes of diffusion and inter-urban flows. Here, McCann (2011) distinguishes between urban policy (formal guidelines and procedures), policy models (general ideas, such as best practices that can be converted into formal policy), and policy knowledge (the expertise about best policies). Policy models can move from one place to another where they are adopted, reworked, and subsequently transmitted to the next place, and so on. Policies flow through urban networks in which some cities are more central—innovator cities that gain favorable attention—and from where policy knowledge and models tend to originate. Each city then "assembles" its own local policy based on non-local knowledge which then becomes "fixed" and shapes local forms of urban development. However, in search for quick solutions, "off-the-shelf" best practices may sometimes be adopted, often due to budget constraints (McCann & Ward, 2012).

Policies circulate among cities by different actors; including local politicians, activists, corporations, scholars, media, non-local organizations, and expert national and international consultants. This circulation is often driven by policy travel, such as fact finding trips and site visits. Innovator cities become destinations with packaged protocols and narratives that they present to incoming visiting delegations (McCann, 2011).

There are numerous case studies of mobility in different policy areas, including drug policy (McCann, 2008), urban design (McCann, 2011), business improvement districts (McCann & Ward, 2013), and urban sustainability (Temenos & McCann, 2012). Recent studies suggest that policy mobilities also take place among music cities. Ross (2017a) reports that Toronto's leadership embarked on a fact finding mission to Austin, Texas and "sung the praises of Austin's live music culture and available spaces for this music culture" (p. 145). Similarly, Baker (2016) identified "city twinning"—formalized partnerships of asymmetric music city knowledge diffusion where one recipient city learns from an innovator city.

3   METHOD

In this chapter, I use the Music Policy Forum as a case study of the circulation of music city policy models and knowledge. MPF is a US-based non-profit organization founded in 2017 and the only one of its kind with an emphasis on North American cities, although it has an international counterpart in the Music Cities Convention, operated by the British-based organization Sound Diplomacy, which has held meetings around the world since 2015, forging global music cities networks. The goal of MPF is to (a) advise decision-makers on music strategies, (b) facilitate meetings and build stakeholder networks, and (c) be a resource for members of music communities (see musicpolicyforum.org). MPF held its first event in Washington DC on October 25–26, 2019. The goal was to explore "the opportunities and challenges facing local music ecosystems" (Music Policy Forum News Release, September 26, 2019). The event was comprised of a private, by invitation only, one-day "intensive," and a second day "summit" open to the public. The first day was attended by 42 people who work with music in creative, educational, or policy-making capacities. According to McCann (2011), policy models and knowledge are transmitted in microspaces, which is "where expertise about globally significant best practice is deployed and discussed, where lessons are learned, where reputations are made" (118–119). A conference like the Music Policy Forum is an example of such a microspace.

To facilitate knowledge transmission, the participants were divided into smaller groups that discussed a pre-determined topic, after which each group shared its ideas and conclusions with the forum at-large. As a participant, I could observe comments and interactions within my assigned group and the subsequent forum-wide sharing of main points, but not all individual group interactions. The latter limited data collection, although not in a way that likely skewed the results. Four roundtable discussions took place during the day, followed by a concluding session. The second day was organized around six panel discussions, with a total of 25 panelists, each followed by a Q&A session from the audience. Most of the first-day attendees were either panelists or were in the audience during the second day.

The MPF organizers set an official discussion agenda for the event and my analysis reflects that agenda. At the same time, the discussion—especially during the first day—was characterized by free-flowing information exchanges that oftentimes deviated significantly from the nominal agenda themes. As a qualitative method that explores the meaning of different forms of communication, I used discourse analysis (see Suciu, 2019) as a tool to thematically organize ideas and arguments that were presented at the MPF. I organized the MPF content into nine themes, which were determined in a post-facto, inductive manner during the data analysis phase after the event.

To study policy mobilities it is important for the researcher to be present where sharing practices take place. McCann (2011) also recommends "ethnographic engagement with participants and processes" (p. 121), especially as "there is remarkably little scholarship on how conferences might be studied ethnographically as research sites, where dispersed communities of policy actors come together in one place" (p. 123). My research design therefore also utilizes participant observation. None of the other participants of the MPF, except the main event organizer, was aware of the fact that I was both a participant and an observer who recorded the discussion in real time during the event. Participant observation is a recognized research method in the social sciences, most commonly practiced among anthropologists and sociologists. It is suitable to investigate social processes that occur within a limited time and place and that cannot easily be studied through some other method (Babbie, 2015). The MPF is precisely such a situation when participant observation can be a useful method.

There are other aspects of participant observation that the researcher must be mindful about (see, e.g., Kawulich, 2005; Brancati, 2018). One is an ethical dilemma: Is it defensible to study people without their explicit consent? The social sciences have answered that question in the affirmative, so long as acceptable levels of privacy and non-disclosure of sensitive material are adhered to (see below). The research results should also have social relevance that outweighs any potential harm to the study subjects (which here can be presumed to be minimal). Another concern is that the process under scrutiny may be affected by comments made and actions taken by the researcher during the participant observation. During the MPF, I did participate in the discussion, although I was consciously limiting such contributions. Issues and ideas that I brought up during the forum have been included in the Analysis section below if they generated some discussion, and if participants agreed that my point of view was valid. In such circumstances, my input has been noted in the text. It is reasonable to assume, though, that my participation did not affect the outcome of the event in any substantial way.

The MPF participants wanted to learn more about music policy; therefore, note-taking during the forum was common, either using pen and paper or a laptop computer. I recorded my observations in real time on a laptop, which was an unobtrusive method that did not disrupt the forum discussion. In fact, my background as a researcher with a scholarly interest in music policy meant that I could seamlessly perform the dual role of a participant and an observer.

The first day of the forum was introduced by the organizer as a "modified off the record" event. The objective of this rule was to ensure that the participants were comfortable sharing proprietary information in a way that facilitated the free exchange of ideas and experiences. On the other hand, the "modified" part also suggests that insights that emerged the forum are ultimately meant to circulate beyond the MPF participants to other stakeholders and the general public.

To anchor my research with the MPF, at the time I accepted the invitation to participate I also sought the approval of the forum organizer. In pre-meeting communication I described my methods and objectives and the project was given a green light so long as no proprietary information was disclosed, no specific individuals could be identified, or potentially sensitive opinions attributed to them. In the Analysis section below, I have therefore identified individuals only as, for example, a "music industry employee from central United States" to conform to privacy expectations, while also contextualize statements and opinions for the reader. Moreover, the Institutional Review Board at my university approved of the research design as described above.

4   ANALYSIS

As music policy meetings are key spaces from where knowledge circulates, the Analysis starts with a brief demographic summary of the meeting participants. The content of the MPF discussion is subsequently analyzed. The data is presented in nine separate (but interrelated) discourses or themes.

4.1   Demographic Background

Figure 3.1 shows both those who attended the first day "intensive" and those who acted as panel discussants during the second day of the event (as noted, some individuals were in both categories). The data is derived from an attendee package that was distributed to the participants. I determined which category each participant belonged to, based on their main professional affiliation.

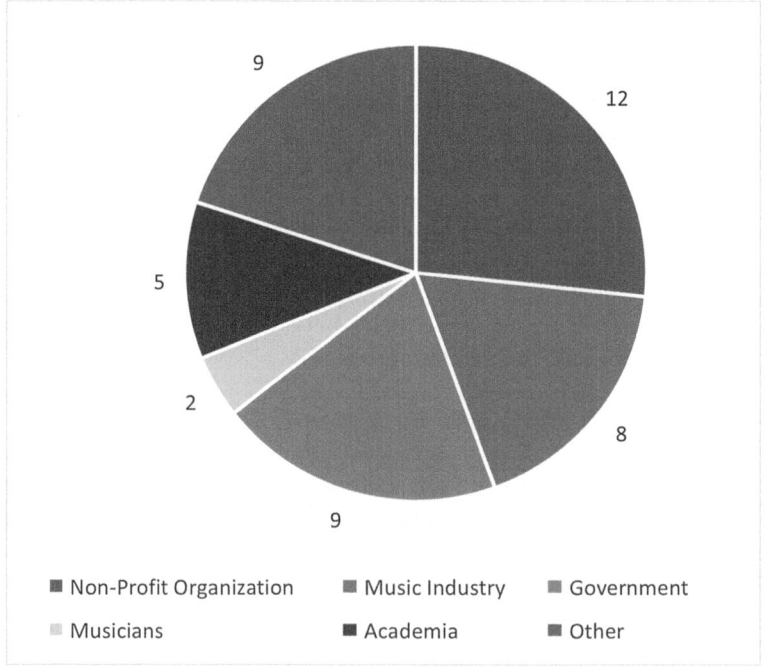

Fig. 3.1   Attendees of the Music Policy Forum, 2019

The MPF demographic is quite broad with representatives from first and foremost non-profit organizations, followed by government and music industry employees. The non-profit organizations are engaged in activities such as supporting musicians, small-scale music industry entrepreneurs, and music education. Music industry is a relatively heterogeneous category with attendees from record labels, music venues, and music industry trade associations. Large transnational music industry actors were conspicuously absent. Instead, the music industry category is dominated by businesses that tend to be active on the local level only. Individuals in the government category are almost exclusively representing city governments, usually holding a position in an office that promotes and manages music, entertainment, arts, and tourism. The "other" category includes individuals employed in media, such as radio, and other small business owners who engage broadly with arts and culture. A smaller number of attendees were academics (not just as researchers but often active in local music ecosystems) and only two musicians (recruited by the organizers to provide a creative perspective). The gender of attendees was relatively well balanced, 56 percent were male and 44 percent female. No data were collected on ethnicity, but a modest number of attendees were Black or of other minorities.

Beyond the Washington DC area, attendees came from cities that are geographically widespread from across North America (Fig. 3.2), including "superstar" music cities such as New Orleans, Seattle, and Austin, and cities that have an active music policy (e.g., Toronto). Cities that are major music industry centers are relatively underrepresented—only one attendee from Los Angeles, one from New York City, and none from Nashville. Out of 45 attendees, 44 were from North America (40 from United States and 4 from Canada), with only 1 from elsewhere (Great Britain).

4.2 Who Are the Stakeholders? (Theme 1)

One of the first steps when formulating a music city policy is to identify a set of stakeholders. Who should be awarded a seat at the table? The MPF organizers presented four elements of a local music ecosystem, as a way to frame stakeholder identification: (1) local government; (2) locally based and music-oriented non-profit organizations; (3) foundations or other entities from whom project funding can be obtained; and (4) music industry and musicians.

Fig. 3.2 The origin of Music Policy Forum participants (excluding one non-North American participant)

Particularly the proper role of government was scrutinized. Through its regulatory and taxation powers, and its service provisions, the local government is inevitably a major stakeholder; however, the forum debate interrogated whether government should be a driver of music policies or acting in a supporting role. No clear consensus emerged among the MPF participants (see Theme 3).

No matter the level of government engagement, as local music ecosystems are metropolitan rather than municipal in scale, coordination between local government entities is desirable. The shared experience at MPF suggests, however, that such coordination is rarely forthcoming. Local government fragmentation is often considered to be an obstacle to efficient policy-making in general (e.g., Rusk, 2013; Miller & Cox, 2014). This is also true for music. As a new policy arena, mechanisms to overcome fragmentation are rarely in place. According to attendees, government entities beyond the main city of a metropolitan area are typically not awarded stakeholder status.

The question of how and if to engage business communities also emerged. A MPF participant from Canada stated that convincing local business to recognize the value of music is important. However, experiences from other cities, as formulated by a West Coast participant, suggest that involving the Chamber of Commerce (or similar organizations) could threaten the credibility of a music city strategy among other stakeholders wary of potential dominance of corporate interests. Those stakeholders would be concerned about potential commodification and dilution of the "authenticity" of music scenes. An East Coast participant echoed such sentiment by labeling a downtown partnership organization "not very useful." The perceived cultural difference between the music ecosystem interests and other economic sectors is often significant (see, e.g., Breen (1993) on the music industry's antipathy toward government intervention, and Johansson (2007) on the complex relationship between the music industry in Nashville and the city's traditional business elite).

As concluded in Demographic Background, forum participants from the music industry represented small music businesses, which is logical considering the capacity building that MPF engages in. Small companies benefit the most from external economies of scale (shared resources in a city that exist outside the boundaries of a firm). At the same time, small businesses and non-profit organizations often develop individual skills that can be transferred to larger companies. Hence, they perform an important role in the ecosystem, and there is a degree of interdependence among different sized actors.

No large corporate actors from the music industry were present at the MPF. During the discussion I voiced that increasing geographic concentration of headquarters into fewer large cities, as documented by the urban governance literature (e.g., Hackworth, 2007), makes corporate culture less place-based than in the past, with fewer historical and personal connections to a specific city. Therefore, corporate entities are less interested in investing resources in the local collective good (Jonas & Wilson, 1999). For example, radio broadcasting is an industry with diminishing local ties, although a Northeastern city found a willing stakeholder in its public radio station that committed to promote local music. One corporate exception mentioned during the MPF discussion came from a participant from a Southern city, who had been able to engage the transnational concert promoter Live Nation.

Finally, musicians are obvious stakeholders; however, the MPF debate conveyed a disconnect between policy-making and artists. Musicians often perceive themselves as creative and atomistic actors and, therefore, not easily organizable (see Theme 6). Most of them are also low income and part-time workers for whom access to housing is a serious concern—the more successful a music city is, the more expensive it tends to be (see

Theme 9)—and as self-employed, health care access among musicians is precarious (see Zendel in this volume). A couple of strategies were suggested during the MPF that could be replicated elsewhere. Non-profits act as advocacy groups for local musicians lobbying for local policies that aim at improving the socio-economic situation of artists. One Canadian city also enacted a policy that musicians must always be paid at city-sponsored events (to avoid the practice where musicians are expected to perform for free at community concerts).

In bringing these different stakeholders together, varied agendas have to be managed. During the process of developing a music city strategy, according to several MPF participants, it becomes apparent who is engaged for the common good, and those who view collective capacity building from a narrow self-interest perspective. The latter becomes "toxic," and it is counterproductive to include them. However, due to the process-oriented and contested nature of stakeholder development, there is no "setlist" formula that can be replicated from one place to another.

4.3   What Is the Appropriate Institutional Structure? (Theme 2)

In conjunction with stakeholder recognition, what type of institutional structure can most effectively promote music city policies? Two such themes were debated during the MPF: (1) the role of local governments (see also Theme 1) and (2) the degree to which music policy is independent vis-à-vis broader cultural policies.

With regards to the governmental question, a series of concerns were raised. Participants noted that with changes in mayoral administrations, enthusiasm for music policy may wax and wane. To paraphrase multiple participants, "it really helps to have a mayor who is a music fan and attends concerts." That implicitly means, though, that it could be hard to sustain policy, which supports the position that music policy should be independent from the executive office. Other forum participants were wary of that conclusion, reflecting different personal experiences on the local level. Here, it is important to recognize that political structures vary (a point I offered during the discussion). The strong mayor in most large American cities has the character of a chief executive officer while in other places, commonly in Europe, the local administrative state may be more important.

If a city considers music policy to be imperative, it can establish a commission/council or a city music government office. MPF participants discussed examples of different administrative structures. Mostly top tier music cites have instituted a music-only administrative unit, as in Portland, Oregon (see musicportland.org). More typical is incorporating music into a creative economy office in city government. Based on the MPF discussion, "nightlife commissions" have increasingly emerged as a way to address concerns around bars, restaurants, and performance venues. The related night mayor concept was first invented in Amsterdam, the Netherlands and has been replicated in cities elsewhere, including in the United States (Seijas & Gelders, 2021). Whatever the exact local structure is, the forum discussants recognized that appointing individuals to policy bodies is an important exercise of power. Who has the capacity to nominate and appoint is determined by both formal and informal power structures. That process overlaps with the identification of stakeholders (see Theme 1), which is inherently a political process that determines whose interests are represented.

4.4   The Formal Music City Plan (Theme 3)

The music city plan is a document that formulates a music strategy, including a set of policy recommendations. The MPF identified approximately 20 North American cities that have a completed a plan or are in the progress of doing so. In some cities, the city is the "lead author" of a music city strategy while in other cases it is one among several ecosystem partners (see Theme 1).

As suggested by the policy mobilities literature, it is common that external experts are contracted to assist with the plan. Sound Music Cities is an Austin-based company that specializes in such reports and is arguably a leader in the field (www.soundmusiccities.com). For example, a Northeastern city represented at the MPF recently published a Sound Music Cities assisted study. The report was described as a collaborative effort among public entities, business interests, and non-profits who wanted to capitalize on a "buzz" around the city in other sectors than music. A key feature of the report is to align resources, both local and non-local, such as state and federal funding opportunities (see Theme 5 on financing).

A representative from a Canadian city shared with the participants that their music report used value chain analysis—a model adopted from business that describes all the actions and resources needed from initial idea to finished "product" (here, a music city plan). The idea of reducing music policy to an economic strategy was met with some resistance though. One participant opined that the writing of formal plans has moved beyond economic impact (i.e., the use of concepts such as multipliers and economic base models); instead, effective communication to encourage stakeholder involvement depends on qualitative persuasion as much as quantitative data.

The MPF revealed some skepticism toward formal plans. The debate ranged from how music plans "collect dust" to cautious but optimistic views on the efficacy of plans. One acknowledged pitfall is when a plan is perceived as an end point. In reality, plan authors learned that a local music community does not immediately embrace their recommendations, which means that post-plan implementation is crucial. Finally, an inherent problem with formal plans is the rapid change of the music industry. Plans operate on a relatively long time frame—one year to complete, and approximately five years for implementation—and may soon become obsolete. Therefore, the music plan should be a system for continuous activation rather than a to-do blueprint.

4.5   *The Data Problem (Theme 4)*

The baseline for a plan is an assessment of resources in a local music ecosystem. MPF participants recognized that national data from the US Bureau of the Census and Bureau of Labor Statistics severely underestimate musicians and the music industry (e.g., inadequate employment categories and under-counted part-time employment). Therefore, music censuses have been conducted in several cities, as inventories of existing resources. Austin, Texas, and cities in Australia and Britain completed some of the first censuses (Titan Music Group, 2015; Behr et al., 2020); now that has been done by several other cities. For example, the Washington DC music census (identified here as it was discussed in the public section of the MPF) elicited 2661 respondents—in itself a sample of all individuals within the DC music ecosystem—which can be compared to about 300 music workers according to national census data. The most common rationale for conducting a local music census is that funding from government and other grant givers require "hard data;" thus, music policymakers must provide a more realistic (and higher) number than national data can provide. Even superstar music cities find it hard to convince governments to invest in music strategies. A census also attempts to tease out the needs of the ecosystem which, according to respondents to the Washington DC census, include more live performance opportunities, advanced education in music management, a more robust local music industry, and improved connectivity within the local music community.

While there is a need for a primer on data, the MPF revealed concerns about the process. Especially among musicians the sentiment is that reports amount to little more than "data for data's sake." Resistance to participate in a census is based on the opinion that collected data will be used "against" the individual; for example, worries about not being funded if they perform the "wrong" kind of music (a perception that popular music is not valued and funded as much as classical music). Moreover, to what extent will the research be of value to marginalized (often Black or minority) communities? Such a concern reflects American skepticism toward government intentions in general. The census-takers' response is that a census is not a "one off"; instead, it should be institutionalized. When established, the value of it may become recognized by the community, and trust established.

4.6   Funding the Music Ecosystem (Theme 5)

As laid out above, funding the music ecosystem is imperative. There is a great degree of place-based variability in terms of the best avenues for funding. Some US states and municipalities have hotel or event ticket taxes that fund grant programs for artistic endeavors, including music-related projects. One non-profit representative from a Midwestern city noted that the institution of such a funding source tripled his budget. Other creative sources include VIP ticket surcharge at music events that is funneled toward local music. A special case is Canada, which has a national cultural support system from broadcasting fees (see Armstrong, 2016).

The MPF unveiled perceived limits to grants and foundation support as means to fund music ecosystem activities: they have their own community enhancing and economic development objectives that only partially overlap with the needs of the music community, grant opportunities may not be available as much for individual artists as for non-profit organizations, and funding may favor visual art over music. The latter could be associated with a generational funding gap—music policy activists are younger than grant giving boards—and the perception is that "high" culture has been favored in the past (see Theme 4). Increasingly, however, popular music is recognized as something of value, economically and culturally. (See van der Hoeven and Hitters in this volume on different types of value of music to cities.) Several MCP participants had in fact been invited by funding groups to review grant proposals that aimed to develop music-related projects.

Beyond traditional grants, music actors can also seek out nontraditional collaborators. One non-profit in a Western city partnered with the city's housing authority to support the development of music facilities for youth. Starting without an established track record, it was a creative way to seek out funding.

4.7   Facilitating Networks and Interaction (Theme 6)

A key goal of the MPF is to encourage networking, both intra-urban and inter-urban—especially the latter is a key from a policies mobility perspective. MPF participants identified the problem with lack of local interaction among music ecosystem actors (see Theme 4). Different music cities were described as "active but fragmented" or "cliquish." The metaphor "silo" was used frequently during the forum.

Networking suggestions in music policy plans to improve communication are often met with wariness among musicians (see Themes 3 and 4). The artist response is usually: We've been networking all along. Why do we need a formal strategy to point that out? However, MPF understood the activities of local musicians and other ecosystem members as an opportunity—examples of grassroots capacity building and networking. For example, DJs in a Southern city created a cartel which in effect set wages at venues. While a grassroots initiative, it is also an example of how further networking—one of the MPF goals—would allow ecosystem members to organize.

Sometimes the MPF participants also critiqued artists for missing the importance of collective action. They opined that artists do not consider the public good; rather, exhibit "what's in it for me" attitudes (see Theme 1). Others contradicted the idea that artists are not sufficiently community-building oriented. In either case, policy-making can "channel the habits" of musicians, meaning that their propensity for constant ad hoc networking may also be helpful collectively in music policy-making.

4.8   Cross- and Upscaling (Theme 7)

Several examples of how local music policy is connected to other places and geographic scales emerged during the MPF, especially policy mobility disseminating from superstar music cites. One West Coast city representative said: My best work on local music policy was by "ripping off" Austin, Texas. Another participant said that his city looked toward Denver as a way to enhance its local scene and to achieve better grassroots organizing. A broader source of inspiration is Richard Florida's arguments about the importance of cultural and creative economies. The music policy community senses that using the Florida discourse can make music-driven development more understandable and attractive to decision-makers.

Further cross-scaling was exemplified by the music strategy of an East Coast city, which started with members of a particular niche scene (jazz music) communicating with their counterparts in another city. Such communication evolved into an understanding about the need to address music policy in a comprehensive manner. Arguably, such cross-scale learning is in its infancy. One participant proposed that MPF could be an ALEC for music policy. ALEC (American Legislative Exchange Council) is a political organization consisting of right-leaning state legislators and corporate interests that successfully writes and disseminates state-level model legislation. According to a local politician in attendance, such an approach can be effective as cities are amenable to ready-made solutions. To reach influential people outside music policy circles, promoting music policy solutions should take place at other cross-scaling sites, such as the US Conference of Mayors.

Local music policies can also be upscaled. One non-profit in a Western city shared its success in obtaining funding from a partnership with a federal agency. Such outcomes can be achieved elsewhere as well. Another form of upscaling is the building of local supportive structures that enabled artists to design tours nationwide, or even internationally.

4.9   Regulatory Obstacles and Reform (Theme 8)

On the ground, music frequently comes into conflict with other land uses and economic interests (see Reia in *New Geographies of Music 2*). This has to be resolved through the regulatory capacity of the city; hence, different regulatory subthemes were addressed at the MPF, such as nuisance and sound ordinances, building codes, and transportation.

Noise pollution is a serious problem for live music. MPF participants suggested that music venues and buskers are easy enforcement targets even if other land uses may be louder. Noise complaints are inevitably based on an element of individual perception with regards to what constitute a disturbance, which may involve a bias against music. Variable enforcement practices are common depending on who the individual ordinance enforcer is. Moreover, noise data tend to not to be comprehensive or available from city offices.

Facing such obstacles, new technology, such as cell phone apps that measure noise levels, can be used by music interests to generate (ideally more favorable) data. Research have found smartphones to be a valuable tool as they are readily available and capable of collecting quality data with a reasonable level of accuracy for basic noise monitoring purposes (Zipf et al., 2020; Leao et al., 2014). Such data may not be formally acceptable by city regulators but nevertheless useful as a starting point for further measurements. Beyond challenging noise complaints, revising noise ordinances is a more thorough strategy. This is possible as noise ordinances are local, while other regulatory obstacles detrimental to the economics of live music, such as liquor permits, tend not to be (see Ballico, 2021). At the MPF, both city successes and failures were discussed. One successful Southern city investigated hundreds of noise ordinances across the United States before they arrived at a locally suitable ordinance. The result has been an investment in venue redesign to mitigate noise and a decline of complaints. In some cities, there are different regulations for venue-dense entertainment districts, while in other cities a noise ordinance is city-wide.

Venues are often housed in adaptive reuse buildings that are not compliant with building codes. This is evident in a history of fires (e.g., Providence, Rhode Island in 2003 and Oakland, California in 2016). The question is then how do you allow for music and other art spaces while also complying with safety standards? One West Coast non-profit participant at the MPF helps artists and musicians to acquire and renovate spaces with the understanding that they must pass the city permit process. Their suggestion is to cultivate a positive relationship with regulatory officials, such as fire marshals. A "nightlife mayor" panelist stressed the importance of compromising with regulatory enforcers and come to reasonable agreements. Ultimately, innovation in music comes from small-scale scenes where DIY and creative spaces play an important role.

Finally, participants concluded that public transit authorities should also be consulted. As venues stay open late at night, asking for extended hours of transit operation is a policy that improves the viability of live music. This is not only an issue for concert goers but also for venue workers. Moreover, better transit can lower alcohol-related accidents. During the MPF, London was cited as an example where such policies had been implemented.

4.10   Music and Gentrification (Theme 9)

Closely related to Theme 8, gentrification can be a threat to music cites. New city center developments bring residents closer to music venues (and occasionally rehearsal space) and a soundscape that they are not familiar with, and may object to. The MPF discussed how Washington DC music stakeholders promoted a new ordinance—an "agent of change" legislation—although ultimately it was not adopted. The agent of change principle is when a "person or business responsible for the change is responsible for managing the impact of the change" (Music Venue Trust, 2014). Originating in Australia (Lee, 2016), it protects existing music venues from new residential development in that it is the new land use (the agent of change) that must mitigate existing potential disturbances (such as soundproofing new buildings so that music from a venue is not too loud—see Theme 8). If agent of change legislation is to be implemented in the United States, it has to be on the local level as land use planning is extremely decentralized, although there are existing precedents, such as right-to-farm laws on the urban fringe that protect farming from regulatory changes that come with residential encroachment. As noted at the MPF, a more limited mechanism to protect venues is when new residents have to sign a waiver where they recognize pre-existing conditions, such as occasionally loud music. In the context of DC, go-go music (a unique regional style of funk) and its soundscape, threatened by gentrification, has created a "don't mute DC" movement, due to fears that the music could disappear (see Mock, 2019). An attendee from a Southern city expressed concerns that fewer children grow up with the culture that created the city's heritage music in the first place, as a result of gentrification (see Woods, 2017). In essence, regulatory hurdles that street music and venues face create a problem for cultural reproduction. In the context of Washington DC, gentrification especially affects Black musicians and music culture negatively. The aforementioned go-go music is associated the city's Black community, which was noted among some individuals in the audience during Day Two. Gentrification in North America is often accompanied with a white-to-Black transition, but depending on the local context, other class and ethnic changes may also impact local music cultures.

Unsurprisingly, venue death was a topic of discussion at the MPF. This concern is also driven by gentrification: older venues give way to "higher and better land use." A participant from a Southern city lamented that an iconic venue was demolished with public money. Participants wished that more political support would be forthcoming; to paraphrase: "the mayor needs to chain himself to the venue and declare 'over my dead body.'" For context, venue death may not always be a decline in the absolute number of music venues, but rather a change in type of venues, ownership patterns, loss of iconic venues, and a change in the location of venues within the urban ecology (see Johansson et al., 2016). A related pressure comes from tourism. In a handful of US cities "overtourism" is a threat. There, local music culture is dislodged by the demands of the visitor economy. When that happens, it is usually in conjunction with gentrification—a new visitors' economy, just like upscale residential developments, are associated with rising rent and both can displace commercial and residential land uses that serves a lower income population, sometimes at the same time and place. Nevertheless, the relative paucity of a discussion of tourism suggests that tourism industry representatives and policy-makers are not well integrated into the stakeholder groups that at least MPF represents (see also Ballico and Bolderman in *New Geographies of Music 2*).

5   Conclusion and Discussion

The Music Policy Forum case study demonstrates how music city policy mobilities are a social process still in its infancy. MPF has only been in existence since 2017 and comprehensive, city-wide music plans, in North America and globally, have mostly been formulated during the last few years. My observation as a participant is that the MPF event was that of a free-flowing exchange of knowledge. The tone was collaborative rather than contentious; the participants were like-minded people interesting in absorbing practices to take home. The debate was characterized by point and counterpoint arguments, which suggests that there is rarely one single policy model to pursue.

Participants came from across North America, but especially from cities that already had a reputation as music cities. They mainly represented music non-profits, small music enterprises, or were local government officials; for all of them MPF was an opportunity to learn about their own role in a local music ecosystem. For some cities, MPF was a way to further develop music policy planning, while for leading music cites participation is also reputation-enhancing as innovator cities from where best practices emanate. Comments from the participants suggest that Austin, Texas is regarded as the preeminent innovator city in music policy.

In this chapter, I identified nine discursive themes, which can be further reduced into four meta-discourses which are, in the language of policy mobilities, precursors to policy models. The first one is the enabling of policy capabilities by identifying and bringing ecosystem stakeholders together and then to facilitate continuous interaction. The second step is the formulation of a strategy—sometimes as a formal planning document underpinned by data collection through a music census. Thirdly, the MPF stressed the identification and acquisition of funding for music ecosystem activities, especially as much of it operates on a non-profit basis. Music policy interests are continuously struggling for recognition as a worthwhile endeavor, both structurally and financially. And finally, music activities on the economic margin face challenges related to urban regulatory practices and increasing land use cost and competition, often in the context of gentrification. Music policy straddles the goals of economic development and building better places, which is a duality that can be both complimentary and contradictory.

Many of the issues raised at MPF mirror conclusions in the literature. While MPF is quite new, policy reports and scholarly research have undoubtedly circulated previously. For example, the notions that music is underfunded compared to other cultural endeavors as it is seen as a market-based activity, not one that ought to be subsidized; policy-makers rarely consult with the night-time professionals when making policies; and musicians are suspicious of public funding, assuming that it is biased, going toward the wrong artists, and dependent on bureaucratic decision-making (e.g., Flew, 2008). Moreover Ross (2017b) points out that music spaces are often not in compliance with zoning, building codes, and other safety standards. Policy mobility microspaces like the MPF have the capacity to disseminate solutions to such challenges. However, the forum does not just provide directly implementable prescriptive measures, but it is also a way for participants to evaluate ideas and formulate what is best practice in their own place-sensitive context.

As an actor in music policy mobilities, the MPF is, according to the organizers, now attempting to position itself organizationally, to act as a funding clearinghouse, to develop a research agenda, and to circulate knowledge. However, a few months after the Washington DC forum, the COVID-19 epidemic exploded around the world. It dramatically affected music city activities—especially those associated with live music and travel. The long-term effects of COVID-19 remain unclear, but it certainly hindered some of MPF's aspirations as face-to-face communication was largely limited to Zoom for some time. The question is also whether COVID-19 fundamentally reshaped local policies and actor relations, or if they will go back to "normal" (i.e., the structures as depicted at MPF)? One way or another, there is need for further research. Such research could focus on the implementation of policy models and knowledge after events like MPF. This chapter focused solely on one microspace of policy mobilities; therefore, extended research may follow how participants assemble insights from an event into local policy.

References

Armstrong, R. (2016). *Broadcasting policy in Canada* (2nd ed.). University of Toronto Press.

Babbie, E. (2015). *The practice of social research* (14th ed.). Cengage Learning.

Baker, A. J. (2016). Music scenes and self branding (Nashville and Austin). *Journal of Popular Music Studies, 28*(3), 334–355.

Baker, A. J. (2017). Algorithms to assess music cities: Case study—Melbourne as a music capital. *SAGE Open, 2017,* 1–12.

Baker, A. J. (2019). *The great music city: Exploring music, space and identity.* Palgrave Macmillan.

Ballico, C. (2021). Caught in the act: The impact of liquor regulation on original live music activity in Perth, Western Australia. *International Journal of Cultural Policy, 27*(3), 394–408.

Ballico, C., & Watson, A. (Eds.). (2020). *Music cities: Evaluating a global cultural policy concept.* Palgrave Macmillan.

Behr, A., Brennan, M., & Cloonan, M. (2020). The UK live music census: The value of researching live music in Glasgow, Newcastle, Oxford, and Beyond. In C. Ballico & A. Watson (Eds.), *Music cities: Evaluating a global cultural policy concept.* Palgrave Macmillan.

Bennett, A., & Peterson, R. (2004). *Music scenes: Local, translocal, and virtual.* Vanderbilt University Press.

Brancati, D. (2018). *Social scientific research.* Sage Publications.

Breen, M. (1993). Making music local. In T. Bennett, S. Frith, L. Grossberg, J. Shepherd, & G. Turner (Eds.), *Rock and popular music: Politics, policies, institutions.* Routledge.

Burke, M., & Schmidt, A. (2013). How should we plan and regulate live music in Australian cities? Learnings from Brisbane. *Australian Planner, 50*(1), 68–78.

Capps, A. (2019). Do cultural plans really help cities save their art and music scenes? *CityLab,* April 10, 2019. Retrieved March 16, 2020, from https://www.citylab.com/life/2019/04/washington-dc-arts-music-scene-cultural-plan-gentrification/586813/

Connell, J., & Gibson, C. (2003). *Sound tracks: Popular music, identity and place*. Routledge.

Flew, T. (2008). Music, cities, and cultural policy: A Brisbane experience. In G. Bloustein, M. Peters, & S. Luckman (Eds.), *Sonic synergies: Music, technology, community, identity*. Ashgate.

Florida, R. (2014). *The rise of the creative class, revisited*. Basic Books.

Gardner, L. (2017). Can city hall make a music scene? *CityLab*, September 12, 2017. Retrieved March 16, 2020, from https://www.citylab.com/life/2017/09/can-city-hall-make-a-music-scene/539436/

Grodach, C. (2013). Cultural economy planning in creative cities: Discourse and practice. *International Journal of Urban and Regional Research, 37*(5), 1747–1765.

Hackworth, J. (2007). *The neoliberal city: Governance, ideology, and development in American urbanism*. Cornell University Press.

Hill, J. (2016). *Country comes to town: The music industry and the transformation of Nashville*. University of Massachusetts Press.

Johansson, O. (2007). Ten people can't run this city anymore: Neoliberalism and governance change in Nashville circa 1987–1999. *Southeastern Geographer, 47*(2), 298–319.

Johansson, O., Gripshover, M. M., & Bell, T. L. (2016). Landscapes of performance and technological change: Music venues in Pittsburgh, Pennsylvania and Nashville, Tennessee. In B. J. Hracs, M. Seman, & T. Virani (Eds.), *The production and consumption of music in the digital age* (pp. 114–129). Routledge.

Jonas, A., & Wilson, D. (Eds.). (1999). *The urban growth machine: Critical perspectives two decades later*. State University of New York Press.

Kawulich, B. (2005). Participant observation as a data collection method. *Forum: Qualitative Social Research., 6*(2), 1.

Kruse, H. (2010). Local identity and independent music scenes, online and off. *Popular Music and Society, 33*(5), 625–639.

Leao, S., Ong, K.-L., & Krezel, A. (2014). 2Loud?: Community mapping of exposure to traffic noise with mobile phones. *Environmental Monitoring and Assessment, 186*, 6193–6206.

Lee, G. (2016). Agents of change in Melbourne's live music scene: A practical review. *INTER-NOISE and NOISE-CON Congress and conference proceedings*. InterNoise16, Hamburg, Germany, pp. 2317–2326.

McCann, E. (2008). Expertise, truth, and urban policy mobilities: Global circuits of knowledge in the development of Vancouver, Canada's 'four pillar' drug strategy. *Environment and Planning A, 40*, 885–904.

McCann, E. (2011). Urban policy mobilities and global circuits of knowledge: Towards a research agenda. *Annals of the Association of American Geographers, 101*(1), 107–130.

McCann, E., & Ward, K. (2012). Assembling urbanism: Following policies and 'studying through' the sites and situations of policy making. *Environment and Planning A, 44*, 42–51.

McCann, E., & Ward, K. (2013). A multi-disciplinary approach to transfer policy research. *Policy Studies, 34*(1), 2–18.

Miller, D., & Cox, R. (2014). *Governing the metropolitan region: America's new frontier*. Routledge.

Mock, B. (2019). How go-go music became kryptonite for gentrification in D.C. *CityLab*, November 18, 2019. https://www.bloomberg.com/news/articles/2019-11-18/go-go-is-the-sound-of-anti-gentrification-in-d-c

Music Venue Trust. (2014). What is 'Agent of Change'…and why is it important? September 11, 2014. Retrieved July 19, 2022, from www.musicvenuetrust.com/2014/09/what-is-agent-of-change-and-why-is-it-important

Pollock, D. (2015). The slow death of music venues in cities. *The Guardian*, 9 September. http://www.theguardian.com/cities/2015/sep/09/the-slow-death-of-music-venues-in-cities?utm_source=SFFB

Ross, S. (2017a). Development versus preservation interests in the making of a music city: A case study of select iconic Toronto music venues and the treatment of their intangible cultural heritage value. *International Journal of Cultural Property, 24*, 31–56.

Ross, S. (2017b). Making a music city: The commodification of culture in Toronto's urban redevelopment, tensions between use-value and exchange-value, and the counterproductive treatment of alternative cultures within municipal legal frameworks. *Journal of Law and Social Policy, 27*, 136–153.

Rusk, D. (2013). *Cities without suburbs: A Census 2010 perspective* (4th ed.). Woodrow Wilson Center Press.

Sánchez Fuarros, I. (2017). "Ai, mouraria!" Music, tourism, and urban renewal in a historic Lisbon neighbourhood. *MUSICultures, 43*(2), 66–88.

Schippers, H. (2015). Applied ethnomusicology and intangible cultural heritage: Understanding 'ecosystems' of music as a tool for sustainability. In S. Pettan & J. T. Titon (Eds.), *Oxford handbook of applied ethnomusicology* (pp. 134–157). Oxford University Press.

Seijas, A., & Gelders, M. (2021). Governing the night-time city: The rise of night mayors as a new form of urban governance after dark. *Urban Studies, 58*(2), 316–334.

Seman, M. (2010). How a music scene functioned as a tool for urban redevelopment: A case study of Omaha's Slowdown project. *City, Culture and Society, 1*(4), 207–215.

Small, A. (2019). Dave Grohl has a pro-rock urban policy agenda. *CityLab*, October 30, 2019. Retrieved March 16, 2020, from https://www.citylab.com/newsletter-editions/2019/10/citylab-daily/601087/

Straw, W. (1991). Systems of articulation, logics of change: Communities and scenes in popular music. *Cultural Studies, 5*(3), 368–388.

Suciu, L. (Ed.). (2019). *Advances in discourse analysis*. IntechOpen.

Temenos, C., & McCann, E. (2012). The local politics of policy mobility. *Environment and Planning A, 44*, 1389–1406.

Terrill, A., Hogarth, D., Clement, A., & Francis, R. (2015). *The mastering of a music city: Key elements, effective strategies, and why it's worth pursuing*. IFPI/ Music Canada.

Titan Music Group. (2015). *The Austin music census: A data-driven assessment of Austin's commercial music economy*. City of Austin Economic Development Department's Music & Entertainment Division.

UNESCO. (2021). *Cities of music network*. Retrieved May 26, 2021, from https://citiesofmusic.net

Urban Land Institute. (2016). *Red River cultural district: Live music preservation*. Special Report, Technical Assistance Panel. ULI.

Wikström, P. (2019). *The music industry* (3rd ed.). Polity.

Woods, C. (2017). *Development drowned and reborn: The blues and bourbon restorations in post-Katrina New Orleans*. University of Georgia Press.

Wynn, J. (2015). *Music/city*. University of Chicago Press.

Zipf, L., Primack, R. B., & Rothendler, M. (2020). Citizen scientists and university students monitor noise pollution in cities and protected areas with smartphones. *PLoS ONE, 15*(9), e0236785.

CHAPTER 4

Centrality and Power in Urban Networks of Music Production: Exploring Relational Geographies in the German Music Market

Kai Marquardt and Christoph Mager

Abstract Popular music emerges in production networks, in which various highly specialized actors such as producers, engineers, and artists interact. Relations between these actors reach out among recording studios across the globe, forming global urban networks of music production. The aim of this chapter is to identify key cities of music production in the German music market in terms of their centrality, power, and position in production networks. Using data on 155 albums of the German Top 20 charts, we apply an approach of social network analysis to identify and map comprehensive global urban networks. Our analysis differentiated by genre, label, and nationality of the artists indicates specific production patterns linking national and international networks thus revealing new relational geographies of music production beyond the dominant Anglophone markets.

K. Marquardt (✉) • C. Mager
Karlsruhe Institute of Technology, Karlsruhe, Germany
e-mail: kai.marquardt@kit.edu; christoph.mager@kit.edu

© The Author(s), under exclusive license to Springer Nature   67
Singapore Pte Ltd. 2023
O. Johansson et al. (eds.), *New Geographies of Music 1*, Geographies
of Media, https://doi.org/10.1007/978-981-99-0757-1_4

Keywords Urban networks • Music industry • Germany • Recording studio • Global city • Social network analysis • Centrality

1   INTRODUCTION

For decades, there has been continued scholarly interest in the organization and repercussions of popular music production. Demand structures, public policies, rights management, organizational restructuring, and—perhaps above all—technological developments constantly shift the conditions of sound production. Since the 1980s, a range of new mediums and file formats for sound storage have transformed the material infrastructure of music products, altering processes of production, dissemination, and consumption. The continuing influence of digital technologies such as cloud storage, streaming services, and platform-based systems of "prosuming" (producing and consuming) has disrupted the structure and business model of the music industry by changing cost structures, modes of reproduction, and market accessibility (Jones et al., 2017). These changes make it difficult to assess or predict impending effects on the structures and spatial organization of the music industry.

Nonetheless, cities continue to play a key role in the geographies of music production. The local development of specific sounds is well documented (Johansson & Bell, 2009), as are the urban origins of various musical genres and scenes (e.g., Emms & Crossley, 2018; Buchholz, 2019). Network perspectives on cities highlight relational aspects of music production, stressing its vertical and horizontal dimensions. The vertical dimension of networks denotes processes between different layers of creativity that connect musicians, formal institutions, and the music industry. These interactions are both preconditions and results of a specific ecology of circulation and negotiation on different geographical scales (Cohendet et al., 2009). The horizontal dimension refers to interactions between individual actors of specific groups, such as musical subcultures or amateur scenes on a more local scale (e.g., Bennett & Peterson, 2004; Makkonen, 2014). Furthermore, taking into account project organization under conditions of globalization, the horizontal dimension of networks stresses the largely trans-local nature of today's professional music production, in which many specialized actors and institutions temporarily interact in global urban networks of recording, mixing, and mastering music. The nodes of this collaboration and transmission are anchored in recording and mastering studios.

By analyzing the spatial and social distribution of these crucial functions within the global city network, the geographies of power relations in the music industry can be better understood. The number and types of network linkages connected to a specific city allow for conclusions to be drawn about the city's role in filtering, managing, and controlling flows of global music production. Building on the seminal work by Watson (2012) on urban networks of production for major Anglophone digital music markets, we perform a social network analysis of studio locations to explore centrality and power in these relational geographies in the German national market. As Watson (2012) observes, there is a relatively scarce number of studies on music production networks outside the Anglophone international music triangle—the UK, the US, and Australia. Analyses of other "regional blocs" (Laing, 1997) or of larger national markets may present a divergent picture of urban connectivity in music production.

In this chapter, we aim to address this research gap by focusing on the German music market. Ranked behind the US and Japan with revenues of 466 million USD (7.7% of the global total value) in 2017, Germany represented the third largest music market in the world (Bundesverband Musikindustrie [BVMI], 2018). Diverging from Watson's (2012) study of the Anglophone digital music markets as represented by iTunes charts, our analysis of the national album charts considers not only digital and streaming revenue but also physical media revenue (i.e., CDs and vinyl shares), which accounts for a significantly higher share in Germany (55%) compared to the Anglophone markets (20%) (BVMI, 2018; Recording Industry Association of America, 2018). Furthermore, we extend the analysis of the overall network by three additional dimensions. Firstly, we analyze the networks of domestic and non-domestic production separately. Secondly, we distinguish between major and independent music companies in the data. Thirdly, we take musical genre as a central decisive factor in our analysis. This slightly de-centered and nuanced approach to the geographies of global production networks accommodates the trajectories and peculiarities of a specific national context. In doing so, we expect to uncover alternative perspectives on the evolution of the economic geography of music (Hracs et al., 2016) beyond the globally dominant Anglophone markets.

In this chapter, we begin with a brief overview of recent organizational and technological changes in music production, highlighting the ability of the music industry to keep power and profit highly concentrated in the hands of a few companies. We illustrate how the economic concentration of power is mirrored in the urban agglomeration of music-related businesses that rely on ecologies of talented musicians, material and institutional infrastructures of music production and consumption, and access to far-reaching networks of skilled workers. Following this, we introduce social network analysis as a tool to measure different aspects of social power and centrality in relational networks. After a brief discussion of methods of data collection and processing, we present the results of our differentiated social network analysis. We conclude by briefly reflecting on the added value of regional analyses of the urban networks of music production and by advocating qualitative studies on networks of popular music production.

2   FROM PRODUCTION LINES TO PROJECT ECOLOGIES: THE CHANGING ORGANIZATION OF THE MUSIC INDUSTRY

In early works on organizational sociology, music production was understood as a multi-stage process that existed within the closed system of a single music firm (Hirsch, 2000). These sequential models of strictly ordered music production were soon questioned by studies that conceptualized musical production as a more collaborative and interactive process (Leyshon, 2001). Different actors in the music industry are actively intervening and changing music, not only by obeying market rationales but also by integrating personal experiences and everyday mediations. Influenced by work in cultural studies that emphasized creativity and consumption, music-making was interpreted as a cultural practice connecting people from within and beyond the recording industry in co-producing cultural content (Negus, 1992).

Cultural studies also acknowledged new contexts by considering subcultures and scenes to be social spaces where production and consumption happen. This shifted the discursive emphasis from the corporate dimension of music production to the diversity of amateur musicking and the complexities of production/consumption. At the same time, the focus on these spaces spurred a greater sensitivity toward the material conditions of local music production by considering rehearsal rooms, venues, studios, or homes (Watson et al., 2009). As a result, several urban scenes with local and interlocal coalitions and alliances between artists, intermediaries, and audiences were identified as birthplaces of new musical genres (Bennett & Peterson, 2004). In these contexts, the concept of the network gained importance in understanding various overlapping and genre-specific webs of music production involving interactions between different actors and institutions (Power & Hallencreutz, 2007; Crossley et al., 2015).

Lorenzen and Frederiksen (2005) conjectured that every music recording is a project that temporarily brings together social actors with different talents and skills in music production. Academic interest soon shifted to this understanding of music production and gradually replaced the focus on intra-firm teamwork (Grabher, 2002; Johansson, 2020). Researchers have also begun to situate projects in their social and organizational context. Temporary project organization that links actors, freelancer, firms, and studios not only yields benefits such as cost savings, flexibility, and specificity but also provides opportunities for building reputations and promoting reflexive learning. New software formats and digital platforms have increasingly lowered the entry barriers to music markets; this has expanded the possibilities of collaborative participation in musical production to actors outside the formal music industry, gradually undermining music firms' historic monopoly on music production and distribution. In sum, the traditional organization of production lines and global production networks of the music industry have been reconfigured into "a complex heterarchical ecology of firms, freelance musicians, online production, and distribution platforms as well as local scenes and online communities engaging in creative content production" (Schiemer et al., 2019, p. 295).

Expanded access to the means of production suggests a democratization of music production. However, recent data on the global music market show that record companies still dominate the global music market economically, with the three largest labels (Sony, Universal, and Warner) retaining about 70% of the global market share (Worldwide Independent Network, 2017). Historically, the music industry has been able to repeatedly adapt to changing conditions (Leyshon, 2014). The ownership of rights that protect the interests in the exploitation of creative work plays a key role in maintaining major labels' market dominance. Licensing across a multitude of platforms and outlets presents a range of revenue opportunities, ranging from performance royalties and mechanical rights for the reproduction of sound carriers to dubbing royalties for the reuse of works. Capital and power are concentrated across the networks of creativity, reproduction, distribution, and consumption and bolster present forms of power (Wikström & DeFillippi, 2016). These steady processes of reconfiguration are especially prevalent on the urban and interurban scales, producing and re-producing asymmetrical geographies of power (Jones et al., 2017).

Across physical space, the activities and loci of the music industry tend to be disproportionately concentrated in urban centers (Scott, 1999; Florida & Jackson, 2010). The three major record companies are anchored in global cities (New York City and Los Angeles/Santa Monica) surrounded by a dense institutional network of smaller record companies, studios, and freelancers in the music business. Agglomeration and urbanization economies are due to lower transaction and infrastructure costs, access to specialized services, proximity to competitors and markets, possibilities of a pool of highly qualified or talented creative workers, and ease of access to global urban networks of music (Power & Jansson, 2004; Hracs, 2012). Urban places where musicians work and live, as well as where social, creative, and cultural infrastructures are well established, act as magnets for other talented musicians (Kloosterman, 2005).

Music production involves a complex system of interactions between many specialized actors and institutions. Those interactions and relationships subsequently form socially and spatially embedded networks of music production (Leyshon, 2001; Crossley et al., 2015). Urban places may, for example, host a unique ecology in which musical knowledge and innovation circulate between different social and spatial scales, from the "underground" of creative individuals to the "middleground" of intermediary groups and communities to the "upperground" of formal institutions and firms (Cohendet et al., 2009). The ability for musicians to create music depends, among other things, on actors like artist and repertoire personnel, producers, and sound engineers, who play important roles as cultural intermediaries or gatekeepers of recording facilities (Hennion, 1989; Horning, 2004). Novel digital technologies may suggest studios' diminishing role in music production (Leyshon, 2014). Nonetheless, these sites still act as centers of creativity and innovation at the highest technological levels, as documented in the detailed listings of studios and other places involved in successful productions (Toynbee, 2016). Accordingly, while music production is concentrated in certain places, it is becoming increasingly dispersed due to digital developments, which is only increasing global connectivity (Florida & Jackson, 2010; Rogers, 2011).

3 MEASURING POWER AND CENTRALITY IN URBAN NETWORKS

From a structural point of view, a city's power can be understood as its ability to dominate other cities in terms of resource availability (Friedmann, 1973). However, power emerging from the relationality of urban networks is much more diffuse—every city holds its own respective position of power in global urban networks (Taylor et al., 2002). An analysis of power in these networks identifies cities that hold favorable positions over others due to their connectivity and, subsequently, their opportunities to participate and influence highly interconnected and interlocking networks (Taylor & Derudder, 2018). Common methods for measuring the roles of different actors in social networks are Bonacich centrality and Bonacich power (Bonacich, 1987). Applied to urban networks, the more central a city, the more links it has to other well-connected cities. Furthermore, the more powerful a city, the more links it has to less-connected cities; these less-connected cities are all the more dependent (Hanneman & Riddle, 2011). Additionally, Freeman's flow betweenness centrality can be applied to assess a city's ability to control information flows—this calculates the centrality of an actor by its participation in flows between all other pairs of actors (Freeman et al., 1991). Cities with a high flow betweenness centrality are often vital in linking poorly connected or unconnected regions in a network (Tabassum et al., 2018). Such cities often act as mediators for their importance in linking different countries or industries. If a city alone assumes the role of central mediator for a particular market, it is referred to as a gatekeeper city because it is decisive in gaining access to a market.

4 DATA COLLECTION AND PROCESSING

All obtained data was based on the locations of recording studios involved in the production of an album, that is, a project. The movement of sounds and information between recording studios engaged with each project linked different cities. Each project creates its own urban network, linking pairs of cities as joint production locations for the album. Analysis that includes multiple projects produces a more comprehensive urban network of music production. The data collection was conducted on a weekly basis from October 2017 to February 2018 based on the top 20 albums on the official German website for music charts (GfK Entertainment GmbH, 2018). Although the analysis of chart-topping albums reflects market preferences and market power rather than being able to provide a complete picture of popular music production networks, this focus has the advantage of comparability with existing studies. Compared to the singles charts, the album charts offer the advantage of more comprehensive information that can be gathered about the various production stages of musical projects. In addition to data on studios and cities involved in recording, mixing, and mastering, information on the artists' origins, genre, and publishing company was collected. The main source for this data was the online database www.discogs.com. Any missing information on individual cases was supplementary researched on the internet.

The final dataset included 155 albums produced in a total of 308 different recording studios in 123 different cities. Roughly half of the albums (n = 75) were German productions, in the sense that either the artist was of German nationality or listed as German (in the case of bands with members of multiple nationalities) on the site discogs.com. International productions were dominated by productions from the US (n = 35) and UK (n = 26). The dataset was then analyzed to gain a general view of the production networks of the German music market on one hand, and to obtain country- and genre-specific insights on the other. The coding of connections between cities was non-directional, so no distinction between "sender" and "receiver" was made. The coded connection data was compiled into a comprehensive, symmetrical 123×123 matrix characterizing the urban networks of music production for the most successful albums of the German music market; additional matrices were made for further analyses by genre, record company, and German versus non-German production. These tables formed the basis for our social network analysis and for mapping the networks of music production. This analysis was done primarily with the software tool UCINET (Borgatti et al., 2002). For geographic visualization, we used the open-source tool Gephi, and for analytical purposes the visualization tool NetDraw (Borgatti, 2002).

5   ANALYSIS

5.1   Global Urban Networks of Music Production According to the German Music Market

Figure 4.1 shows a non-geographic representation of the urban networks of music production according to the German music charts, demonstrating the embeddedness of individual cities. Los Angeles and New York each

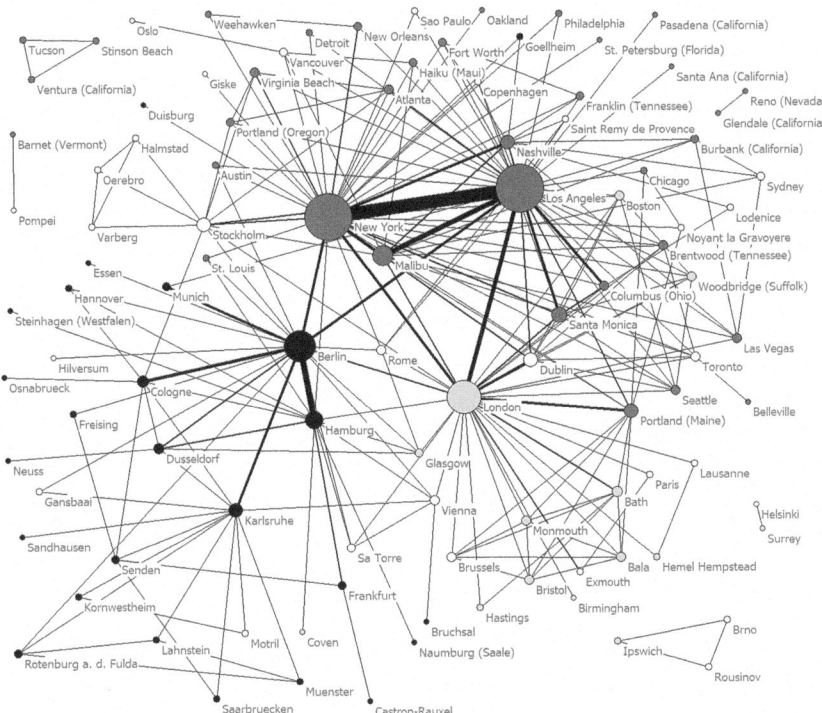

Fig. 4.1 The connectivity of cities in urban networks of music production in the German music market. Note: The size of each node is determined by the total number of a city's connections. The thickness of the line linking two cities is based on how often the pair was joint production sites for an album. The country of each city is represented by node shade (black for Germany, dark gray for the US, light gray for the UK, and white for other countries). Isolated cities (n = 20) are not represented in this figure

had the highest number of connections in the network (n = 73 and n = 70, respectively) and they also had the most connections between them of any linked pair (n = 17). Berlin and Hamburg were the most connected cities in Germany (n = 43 and n = 21, respectively) but had significantly fewer connections. As joint production sites for eight albums, they form the second most strongly interconnected dyad in the network. The figure also shows a relatively high density of intranational urban links and a lower density of international connections.

Berlin and Hamburg were also the most productive German cities to generate successful albums in Germany, as demonstrated by their album outputs. An album is considered to be an output of a city as soon as a recording studio located in the specific city becomes involved in the production process. Recording studios in Berlin were involved in more than a fifth of all albums (n = 34), closely followed by Los Angeles (n = 32), New York (n = 27), London (n = 22), and Hamburg (n = 19). Los Angeles, New York, and London are well known for their importance as traditional centers for economic and cultural developments. They are historically well connected and offer large potential markets, both optimal conditions for an expanding music industry (Baker, 2019). Not quite on this scale, but similar in principles, Berlin as the largest and capital city of Germany forms a central place for the German music industry. However, Hamburg was the city with the greatest importance for music production in Germany until the 1990s. On the one hand, the major labels PolyGram (later Universal) and Warner Music, as well as important German labels of niche production had their headquarters in Hamburg. On the other hand, Hamburg was the origin of innovative and influential pop music styles, such as the so-called Hamburger Schule and Hamburg hip-hop (Kuchar, 2014). Today, the headquarters of Universal Music are located in Berlin, while Warner Music remains in Hamburg.

In Fig. 4.2, the same global urban network of music production is mapped geographically. The figure demonstrates that Germany's top albums were produced almost exclusively in countries of the Global West, particularly in Germany, the US, and the UK. Especially surprising are the results for three German cities: Munich, Cologne, and Karlsruhe. Cologne and in particular Munich, although recognized as top centers of media production within Europe (Krätke & Taylor, 2004), do not play a central role in the networks of music production. This reflects their primary role as central nodes in networks of media production in general, especially in areas of film and television production (Bathelt & Gräf, 2008; Hoyler & Watson, 2019). Karlsruhe presents a special case that will be discussed later.

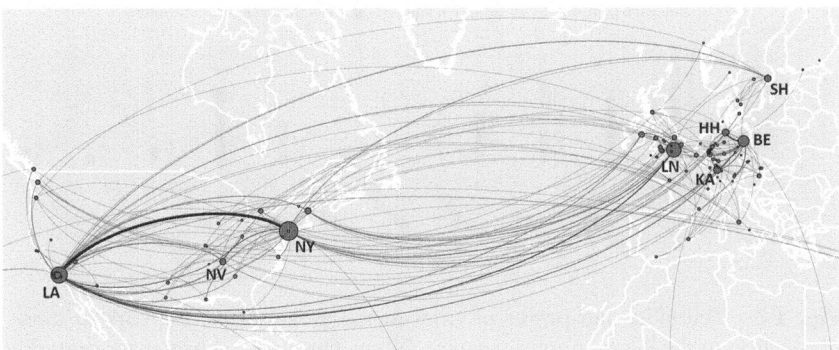

Fig. 4.2 Global urban networks of music production in the German music market. Note: The size of each node is relative to the total number of a city's connections. The thickness of the line linking two cities is based on how often the pair was joint production sites for an album. City codes: BE—Berlin, HH—Hamburg, KA—Karlsruhe, LA—Los Angeles, LN—London, NV—Nashville, NY—New York, SH—Stockholm

5.2 Role Play in Urban Networks of Music Production: The Centrality and Power of Cities

Figure 4.3 shows, in descending order, the top 12 cities measured by Bonacich centrality. Los Angeles and New York have the highest values for both centrality and power, as they also accounted for the highest numbers of connections in the network. Berlin ranks third in terms of Bonacich centrality measure, meaning it is the most central and powerful German city in the global network of music production. Hamburg is the second most central city in Germany. The data indicates a strong correlation between Bonacich centrality and Bonacich power—the most central cities also seem to be the most powerful, indicating a historical path dependency on global actors in established networks of music production.

However, Freeman's flow betweenness centrality conveys a somewhat different picture of the power structures. Particularly striking are the high deviations of flow betweenness centrality from Bonacich centrality for Stockholm and the German city of Karlsruhe. While Stockholm has many international connections, other Swedish cities are only connected nationally. This demonstrates the important position Stockholm assumes as an international gatekeeper for the Swedish music industry. Karlsruhe's high flow betweenness centrality value suggests that it has a high potential for

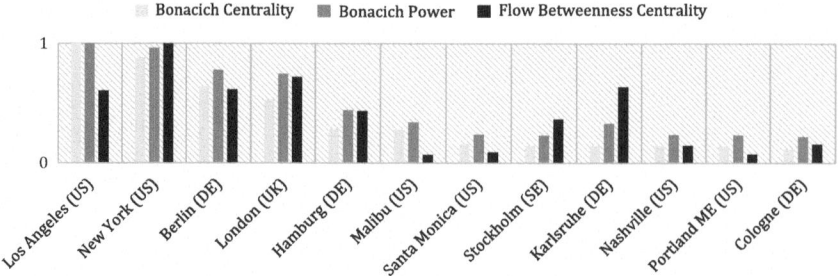

Fig. 4.3 Centrality and power of cities in the global urban network of music production in the German music market. Note: This figure shows three centrality measures for the 12 cities with the highest Bonacich centrality values, in descending order. All values are relative to the highest value of a specific centrality measure

taking on a similar mediating role for Germany. However, it is actually Berlin that serves as the German music industry's gatekeeper—the capital city clearly has more connections to international cities than any other German city. In contrast, over 80% of Karlsruhe's direct connections were to other German cities. All 11 albums that were co-produced in the city were mastered there, 10 of which were done at one particular studio, 24-96 Mastering. This makes 24-96 Mastering the studio most involved in the production of successful music in Germany by far. Since mastering is a process that can be understood as a directed movement, recordings are often sent to a small number of studios for mastering, which are thus involved in a disproportionate share of projects (Watson, 2015). Karlsruhe can be viewed as a "receiver city," into which urban networks of music production begin to converge. A similar pattern was found for the case of Portland (Maine) in the Anglophone market (Watson, 2012).

5.3   Local Roots and Shifting Structures in Global Networks of Music Production: An International Comparison of Domestic Production Patterns

In comparison to the Anglophone markets, urban networks of the German music market are much less concentrated in single cities and less likely to be dominated by a small number of recording studios. This reflects Germany's polycentric spatial structure, within which economic functions are distributed among many agglomeration areas of different sizes (Hoyler,

2011). Global cities like Los Angeles, New York, or London dominated Anglophone music production as joint production sites for more than 40% of all successful albums. Select recording studios like Sterling Sound in New York were involved in more than 20% of all successful productions (Watson, 2012). In comparison, the German music market was dominated by Berlin, which served as a joint production site for just 22% of all albums. The recording studios with the greatest numbers of outputs, Sterling Sound and 24-96 Mastering, each accounted for only about 6% of all albums.

An analysis of the networks of German and non-German productions reveals significant differences. German networks are largely domestically oriented, centering on the Berlin-Hamburg dyad (see Fig. 4.4). While the UK/US production network rarely involves German cities, the German

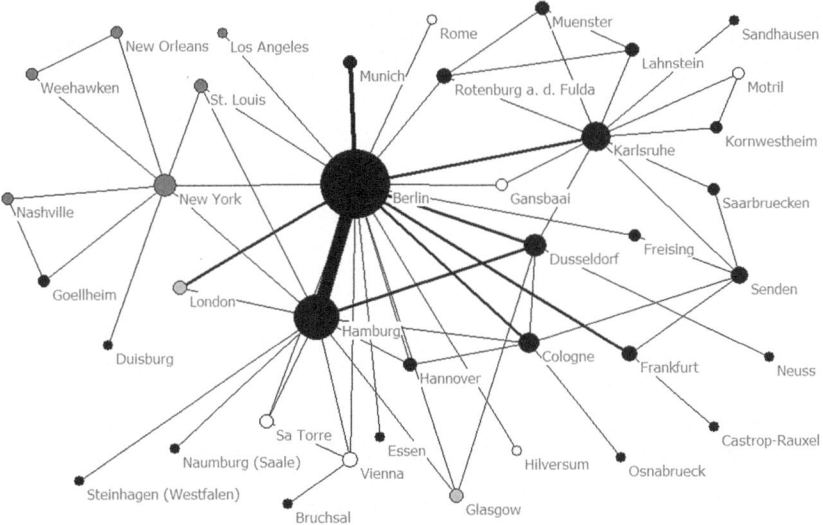

Fig. 4.4 Urban networks of German music production. Note: The size of each node is determined by the total number of a city's connections. The thickness of the line linking two cities is based on how often they were joint production sites for an album. The country of each city is represented by node color (black for Germany, dark gray for the US, light gray for the UK, and white for other countries). Isolated cities (n = 15) are not represented in this figure

production network includes several cities from the US and the UK. Most international cities such as Los Angeles and London are by far not as central and powerful for German music production as they were for UK/US production. The exception is New York, which has a high flow betweenness centrality value that indicates the city's role as a mediator between the German and the US industries.

German music production is more internationally oriented than US music production but less internationally oriented than the UK market. The share of foreign cities in the German networks is about 30%, while for the US and the UK it is roughly 15% and 65%, respectively. This illustrates the dominance of the US industry. Artists from the US tend to stay in their home country and are rooted in primarily national production networks, whereas non-US artists more often seek out international locations as well. These include, above all, connections to the US music industry, as the data in the UK and Germany cases indicate. Furthermore, German productions are much more locally orientated than UK/US productions. This is shown by the network's lower overall density, the number of albums exclusively produced in one city (single-city productions) and the large number of isolated cities in the network (see Table 4.1).

In sum, Berlin and Hamburg dominate the networks of German music production—they host the largest numbers of the record companies involved in producing Germany's top 20 albums. At the same time, these cities are home to the largest numbers of musicians in Germany (Stiller et al., 2014). Thus, even if the urban networks are rather decentralized compared to those in the UK or US markets, agglomeration and urbanization economies strongly affect the German music industry.

Table 4.1 Network properties—German production and UK/US production

	Overall network	*German production*	*UK/US production*
Albums	155	75	62
independent/major label	70/85	47/26	19/43
Cities	123	54	67
from DE/UK/US	38/36/16	38/6/2	3/32/15
Single-city productions	54	33	14
Isolated cities	20	15	3

5.4 Labeled Networks: Local or Global—It's a Thing of Resources and Dominance

Table 4.2 offers some characteristics of the networks of music production differentiated by major labels and independent labels. The three major music companies considered are Warner Music, Sony Music, and Universal Music, each encompassing their respective subsidiary labels as well. Independent labels accounted for a significantly lower network density and a higher number of single-city productions compared to the major labels. Their geographic reach tended to be less extensive and more diverse. This may be due to limited financial resources and a tendency to preferentially cater to niches in the music market (Benner & Waldfogel, 2016). In contrast, urban networks of music production seem to benefit from the opportunities offered by major companies. These labels are geographically concentrated in the cities most active in music production on both a global scale—such as London, Los Angeles, and New York—as well as on a national scale—including Berlin and Hamburg—forming highly interconnected networks. However, the data bias must be taken into account. While this picture is evident for the most successful music in Germany, local productions and the location of music that did not make it into the top 20 are not considered here.

5.5 Genre-Specific Cultures and Networks of Music Production

According to Negus (2013), genres like rock, pop, country, or hip-hop each have sets of musical features and events governed by specific rules concerning the social, commercial, and spatial organization of music production. The most common genres in music production are rock and pop. As they jointly accounted for a high proportion of all analyzed albums for

Table 4.2 Network characteristics—major labels and independent labels

	Major labels	Independent labels
Albums	85	70
DE/UK/US productions	28/17/25	47/9/10
Cities	84	67
from DE/UK/US	18/12/29	29/6/14
Single-city productions	23	27
Isolated cities	10	15

this study, their network patterns mirror those of the overall network. However, these patterns diverge for the genres of hip-hop and country. We selected the two genres due to the fact that they could be clearly separated in the data set. This means that no album of the genre hip-hop could be assigned to the genre country at the same time, and vice versa. Our dataset includes 26 hip-hop (21 domestic, five non-domestic) and 11 country (four domestic, seven non-domestic) albums. Although the sample size for country was less than half that of hip-hop, there were 25 different cities in the broader network for country music production. Meanwhile, hip-hop's network consisted of only 20 cities (see Figs. 4.5 and 4.6). The structure of the urban networks of country music production shows strong patterns of domestic production that link together only a few cities, like London or Portland (Fig. 4.5). These networks are largely decentralized, lacking an identifiable set of core cities. These findings are further substantiated by each city's values for Bonacich centrality and Bonacich power, as well as flow betweenness centrality. London, Portland, and New York lead all three categories with values that are narrowly

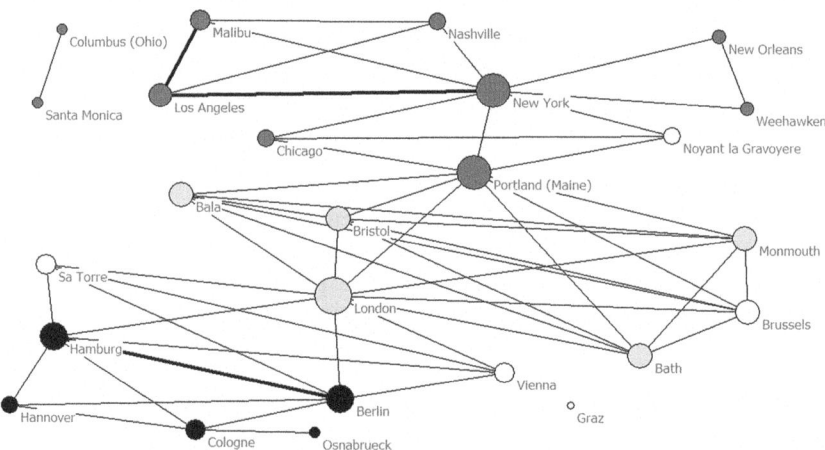

Fig. 4.5 Urban networks of country music production. Note: The size of each node is determined by the total number of a city's connections. The thickness of the line linking two cities is based on how often the pair was joint production sites for an album. The country of each city is represented by node color (black for Germany, dark gray for the US, light gray for the UK, and white for other countries). Isolated cities are included here

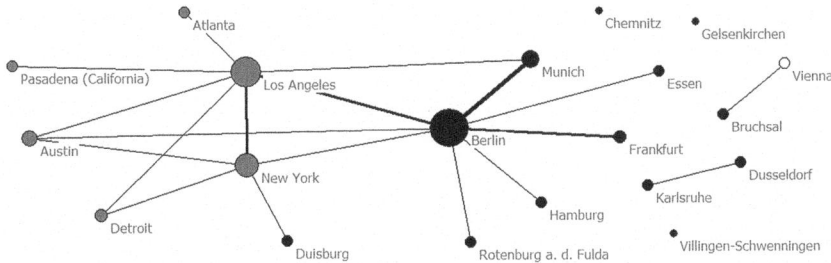

Fig. 4.6 Urban networks of hip-hop music production. Note: The size of each node is determined by the total number of a city's connections. The thickness of the line linking two cities is based on how often the pair was joint production sites for an album. The country of each city is represented by node shade (black for Germany, dark gray for the US, light gray for the UK, and white for other countries). Isolated cities are included here

distinguished. Portland, Maine is a special case in point, as all albums produced there were country albums that involved a single mastering studio, Gateway Mastering. Although Portland has the highest value of flow betweenness centrality, it might not be considered a gatekeeper for the UK and US industries considering its "receiver" role. This corroborates Watson's (2012) research, for Portland is significant in music production because of a single studio at which networks converge—just as is the case with Karlsruhe for the German music industry.

In contrast, our data demonstrate that urban networks of hip-hop music production are clearly dominated by Berlin. The city served as a production location for half of all albums and had direct connections to nearly 50% of all other cities in the genre-specific sub-network (Fig. 4.6). Munich and Berlin were the most strongly connected of all city pairs in German hip-hop production. However, the overall network density is significantly low, and more than a third of all hip-hop albums were single-city productions. Comparatively speaking, these projects are rather locally orientated; this reflects the culture of hip-hop music production, which is often organized around small and informal communities or artists' own independent labels (Mager, 2007; Harkness, 2014; see also Guillard in this volume for a comparison with the hierarchy of French hip-hop cities). The results confirm that music genres tend to form unique cultures that result in specific socio-spatial networks of music production. Since about 80% of the hip-hop albums were domestic productions, these findings corroborate that German music production by itself is increasingly forming local networks.

6   CONCLUSION: EVOLVING ECONOMIC GEOGRAPHIES OF MUSIC BEYOND THE DOMINANT ANGLOPHONE MARKETS

Popular music is increasingly a product of temporary interactions between record company personnel, artists, and highly specialized actors such as producers and sound engineers. These mutual relationships form complex networks of creative co-production that are spatially anchored in places equipped with sound technologies for recording, mixing, and mastering. These loci, mostly found in cities, benefit from agglomeration and urbanization economies due to wider access to network infrastructures and talent pools. Advances in digital technologies enable international teams to collaborate on music production on a global scale. While music can be produced across the globe, certain locations, studios, and specialists are more often involved in production projects than others. Previous analyses have revealed power geometries in the global networks of music production for the most dominant Anglophone markets. In our analysis, we focused instead on the German popular music market, which in 2017 represented the third largest global market in terms of revenue with a domestic share of about 55%. We also refined our analysis according to include musical genre, record company size, and the origin of music production.

The urban networks of music production in the German market are influenced by global network structures but have some unique features. These include the powerful dyad of Berlin and Hamburg that mirrors that of Los Angeles and New York, but on a smaller scale. In particular, Berlin acts as a gatekeeper city by mediating between different international music industries. Karlsruhe, Stockholm, and Hamburg show new relational patterns on the periphery of the global urban network; these cities mediate between and within national industries. The case of Karlsruhe—as a city disproportionately involved in projects due to a specialization—demonstrates a concentration of production functions in a peripheral city. Conversely, Munich and Cologne, which are known to be large European media production centers, hold secondary positions in the network of music production.

Our analyses that differentiated between domestic/non-domestic productions, independent/major networks, and genre types revealed more nuanced geographies that reflect specific trajectories in the German context. The data that parsed the origins of production showed that German networks are decentralized and locally orientated relative to international production networks which reflect the polycentric and functionally differentiated structure of the German urban system. Furthermore, the data for successful independent albums on the German market illustrated that they tend to have a narrower, yet more diverse, geographic reach than major production networks. Against the backdrop of findings on increasing shares of domestic music in many Western music markets (Bekhuis et al., 2014) and an intensification of multidirectional musical flows (Verboord & Brandellero, 2018), this raises questions about the extent to which national specificities of musical production networks might have an impact on the geometries of global networks. Finally, our analysis differentiated by genre pointed to the significance of historic and geographic development trajectories of local and trans-local scenes in music production networks. This is particularly evident in the case of hip-hop music. There is room for research that examines in further detail the role of niche scenes and genre-specific cultures for music production networks in the urban setting.

Our results also raise questions on how exactly production networks arise and how local and urban policies might have an impact on the role of a city in increasingly heterarchical and multi-scalar arrangements. Future studies should integrate qualitative research approaches, like interviews with local actors, not only artists and engineers, but also cultural mediators such as "night mayors," commissioners for pop culture, and other cultural agents. Such studies might help to better understand the role of cultural governance for local scenes and more place-specific networks of successful single-city productions. Furthermore, ambitions for strategically positioning a city in a global network of music production could be scrutinized by eliciting the city's participation in international music fairs and the embeddedness of institutional stakeholders in cultural and media policy networks on different spatial scales (see Johansson in this volume). Our findings suggest that stages of the production process, especially mastering, are located in comparatively few urban centers or rather peripheral locations. This opens up questions about specific contexts and doings of multi-local production, which may depend not only on managerial decisions or on the reputation of single studios but also on biographical backgrounds and individual preferences of engineers, musicians, and music industry personnel.

References

Baker, A. (2019). *The great music city: Exploring music, space and identity*. Palgrave Macmillan.

Bathelt, H., & Gräf, A. (2008). Internal and external dynamics of the Munich film and TV industry cluster and limitations to future growth. *Environment and Planning A, 40*(8), 1944–1965.

Bekhuis, H., Lubbers, M., & Ultee, W. (2014). A macro-sociological study into the changes in the popularity of domestic, European, and American pop music in Western Countries. *European Sociological Review, 30*(2), 180–193.

Benner, M. J., & Waldfogel, J. (2016). The song remains the same? Technological change and positioning in the recorded music industry. *Strategy Science, 1*(3), 129–147.

Bennett, A., & Peterson, R. A. (2004). *Music scenes: Local, translocal and virtual*. Vanderbilt University Press.

Bonacich, P. (1987). Power and centrality: A family of measures. *American Journal of Sociology, 92*(5), 1170–1182.

Borgatti, S. P. (2002). *NetDraw software for network visualization*. Analytic Technologies.

Borgatti, S. P., Everett, M. G., & Freeman, L. C. (2002). *Ucinet 6 for windows: Software for social network analysis*. Analytic Technologies.

Buchholz, M. (2019). Organizations, institutions and networks in local scenes: The growth of San Francisco Bay Area punk rock. *Geoforum, 103*, 158–166.

Bundesverband Musikindustrie. (2018). *Global music report 2017*. Retrieved December 18, 2020, from https://www.musikindustrie.de/fileadmin/bvmi/upload/06_Publikationen/GMR/GMR2018.pdf

Cohendet, P., Grandadam, D., & Simon, L. (2009). Economics and the ecology of creativity: Evidence from the popular music industry. *International Review of Applied Economics, 23*(6), 709–722.

Crossley, N., McAndrew, S., & Widdop, P. (2015). Introduction. In N. Crossley, S. McAndrew, & P. Widdop (Eds.), *Social networks and music worlds* (pp. 1–13). Routledge.

Emms, R., & Crossley, N. (2018). Translocality, network structure, and music worlds: Underground metal in the United Kingdom. *Review of Sociology/Revue canadienne de sociologie, 55*(1), 111–135.

Florida, R., & Jackson, S. (2010). Sonic city: The evolving economic geography of the music industry. *Journal of Planning Education and Research, 29*(3), 310–321.

Freeman, L. C., Borgatti, S. P., & White, D. R. (1991). Centrality in valued graphs: A measure of betweenness based on network flow. *Social Networks, 13*(2), 141–154. https://doi.org/10.1016/0378-8733(91)90017-N

Friedmann, J. (1973). The spatial organization of power in the development of urban systems. In L. S. Bourne & J. W. Simmons (Eds.), *Systems of cities* (Vol. 4, pp. 328–340). Oxford University Press.

GfK Entertainment GmbH. (2018). *Offizielle Deutsche charts.* Retrieved August 1, 2018, from https://www.offiziellecharts.de/

Grabher, G. (2002). Cool projects, boring institutions. Temporary collaboration in social context. *Regional Studies, 36*(3), 205–214.

Hanneman, R. A., & Riddle, M. (2011). Concepts and measures for basic network analysis. In J. Scott & P. J. Carrington (Eds.), *The SAGE handbook of social network analysis* (pp. 340–369). Sage.

Harkness, G. (2014). Get on the mic: Recording studios as symbolic spaces in rap music. *Journal of Popular Music Studies, 26*(1), 82–100.

Hennion, A. (1989). An intermediary between production and consumption: The producer of popular music. *Science, Technology, & Human Values, 14*(4), 400–424.

Hirsch, P. (2000). Cultural industries revisited. *Organization Science, 11*(3), 356–361.

Horning, S. (2004). Engineering the performance: Recording engineers, tacit knowledge and the art of controlling sound. *Social Studies of Science, 34*(5), 703–731.

Hoyler, M. (2011). External relations of German cities through intra-firm networks—A global perspective. *Raumforschung und Raumordnung, 69*(3), 147–149.

Hoyler, M., & Watson, A. (2019). Framing city networks through temporary projects: (Trans)national film production beyond 'Global Hollywood'. *Urban Studies, 56*(5), 943–959.

Hracs, B. (2012). A creative industry in transition. The rise of digitally driven independent music production. *Growth and Change, 43*(3), 442–461.

Hracs, B. J., Seman, M., & Virani, T. E. (2016). Introduction. The evolving economic geography of music. In B. J. Hracs, M. Seman, & T. E. Virani (Eds.), *The production and consumption of music in the digital age* (pp. 3–8). Routledge.

Johansson, O. (2020). *Songs from Sweden: Shaping pop culture in a globalized music industry.* Palgrave Macmillan.

Johansson, O., & Bell, T. L. (2009). *Sound, society, and the geography of popular music.* Ashgate.

Jones, C., Lorenzen, M., & Sapsed, J. (2017). Creative industries. A typology of change. In C. Jones, M. Lorenzen, & J. Sapsed (Eds.), *The Oxford handbook of creative industries* (pp. 3–30). Oxford University Press.

Kloosterman, R. (2005). Come together: An introduction to music and the city. *Built Environment, 31*(3), 247–257.

Krätke, S., & Taylor, P. J. (2004). A world geography of global media cities. *European Planning Studies, 12*(4), 459–477.

Kuchar, R. (2014). Musikproduktion in Hamburg—Musikalische Akteure im Spannungsfeld von Künstlerexistenz und neoliberaler Stadtentwicklung. In A. Barber-Kersovan, V. Kirchberg, & R. Kuchar (Eds.), *Music City: Musikalische Annäherungen an die kreative Stadt* (pp. 217–244). transcript.

Laing, D. (1997). Rock anxieties and new music networks. In A. McRobbie (Ed.), *Back to reality? Social experience and cultural studies* (pp. 116–132). Manchester University Press.

Leyshon, A. (2001). Time–space (and digital) compression: Software formats, musical networks, and the reorganisation of the music industry. *Environment and Planning A: Economy and Space, 33*(1), 49–77.

Leyshon, A. (2014). *Reformatted: Code, networks, and the transformation of the music industry.* Oxford University Press.

Lorenzen, M., & Frederiksen, L. (2005). The management of projects and product experimentation: Examples from the music industry. *European Management Review, 2*(3), 198–211. https://doi.org/10.1057/palgrave.emr.1500044

Mager, C. (2007). *HipHop, Musik und die Artikulation von Geographie.* Steiner.

Makkonen, T. (2014). Tales from the thousand lakes: Placing the creative network of metal music in Finland. *Environment and Planning A: Economy and Space, 46*(7), 1586–1600.

Negus, K. (1992). *Producing pop. Culture and conflict in the popular music industry.* Edward Arnold.

Negus, K. (2013). *Music genres and corporate cultures.* Routledge.

Power, D., & Hallencreutz, D. (2007). Competitiveness, local production systems and global commodity chains in the music industry. *Regional Studies, 41*(3), 377–389.

Power, D., & Jansson, J. (2004). The emergence of a post-industrial music economy? Music and ICT synergies in Stockholm, Sweden. *Geoforum, 35*(4), 425–439.

Recording Industry Association of America. (2018). *RIAA releases 2017 year-end music industry revenue report.* Retrieved December 18, 2020, from https://www.riaa.com/riaa-releases-2017-year-end-music-industry-revenue-report/

Rogers, A. (2011). Butterfly takes flight: The translocal circulation of creative practice. *Social & Cultural Geography, 12*(7), 663–683.

Schiemer, B., Schüßler, E., & Grabher, G. (2019). Collaborative innovation online: Entanglements of the making of content, skills, and community on a songwriting platform. In J. Sydow & H. Berends (Eds.), *Managing interorganizational collaborations: Process views* (pp. 293–316). Emerald.

Scott, A. J. (1999). The US recorded music industry: On the relations between organization, location, and creativity in the cultural economy. *Environment and Planning A: Economy and Space, 31*(11), 1965–1984.

Stiller, S., Wedemeier, J., & Felkers, B. (2014). Die Musikwirtschaft in Hamburg—Status Quo und Entwicklungstrends. In A. Barber-Kersovan, V. Kirchberg, &

R. Kuchar (Eds.), *Music City. Musikalische Annäherungen an die kreative Stadt* (pp. 289–306). transcript Verlag.

Tabassum, S., Pereira, F. S., Fernandes, S., & Gama, J. (2018). Social network analysis: An overview. *WIREs data mining knowledge discovery, 8*, e1256.

Taylor, P. J., & Derudder, B. (2018). Exploring the world city network. In J. Harrison & M. Hoyler (Eds.), *Doing global urban research* (pp. 34–51). Sage.

Taylor, P. J., Walker, D. R., Catalano, G., & Hoyler, M. (2002). Diversity and power in the world city network. *Cities, 19*(4), 231–241.

Toynbee, J. (2016). *Making popular music. Musicians, creativity and institutions.* Bloomsbury.

Verboord, M., & Brandellero, A. (2018). The globalization of popular music, 1960–2010: A multilevel analysis of music flows. *Communication Research, 45*(4), 603–627.

Watson, A. (2012). The world according to iTunes: Mapping urban networks of music production. *Global Networks, 12*(4), 446–466.

Watson, A. (2015). *Cultural production in and beyond the recording studio.* Routledge.

Watson, A., Hoyler, M., & Mager, C. (2009). Spaces and networks of musical creativity in the city. *Geography Compass, 3*(2), 856–878.

Wikström, P., & DeFillippi, R. (2016). *Business innovation and disruption in the music industry.* Edward Elgar.

Worldwide Independent Network. (2017). *Worldwide independent market report 2017.* Retrieved December 18, 2020, from https://winformusic.org/wintel/wintel-2017/

Local Scenes, National Industry, and Virtual Platforms: Overcoming Spatial Hierarchies in French and American Rap Music (2000–2015)

Séverin Guillard

Abstract In France as in the US, music practices have long been structured by spatial hierarchies between cores and peripheries. Scholars have addressed this issue through two main perspectives: economic geographers have analyzed the irregular distribution of music infrastructures on a national scale, while popular music researchers have focused on local music scenes, and on how artists defend the "authenticity" of a genre in localized contexts. However, there have not been many studies on how hierarchies among music scenes are perpetuated, how artists are influenced by these hierarchies, and how they can overcome them to build their careers. In this chapter, I will address these issues by analyzing the evolving role of two local scenes: the urban regions of Atlanta (United States)

S. Guillard (✉)
University Picardie Jules Verne, Amiens, France
e-mail: severin.guillard@u-picardie.fr

© The Author(s), under exclusive license to Springer Nature
Singapore Pte Ltd. 2023
O. Johansson et al. (eds.), *New Geographies of Music 1*, Geographies
of Media, https://doi.org/10.1007/978-981-99-0757-1_5

and Lille (France), from 2000 to 2015. Despite originally having a similar status within French and American rap hierarchies, Atlanta and Lille followed diverging paths: while Atlanta became a new hotbed for the genre, Lille remained at the industry's margins. I will show that these dissimilarities can be explained by differences in the structure of the music industry in each country, the image of the local scene conveyed in music songs and videos, and the ways artists have leveraged local resources in their careers. Far from changing core-periphery patterns, the rise of a virtual platform has reinforced this dichotomy as artists employ them differently. Therefore, I will argue that Lille and Atlanta provide a unique lens to highlight the power relations which influence artists' careers in French and American music industries, and how they are reconfigured with the rise of new digital resources.

Keywords Local scene • Music industry • Virtual platforms • Rap music • Scales • France • United States

1   Introduction

In 1995, Madison Square Garden in New York was the site of the second edition of the Source Music Awards, organized by the main US hip-hop magazine. While the event was dominated by tensions between East and West Coast rappers, with representatives of each claiming to dominate the rap "game," it also highlighted understated geographical inequalities in the rap industry. Against all odds, the award for the best new group was given to an up-and-coming duo from Atlanta: Outkast. The group was booed while on stage, as many attendees contested the award attribution to a group located outside the two main rap regions. This led one of the group's members, Andre 3000, to declare in his acceptance speech, "I'm tired of close minded folks … It's like we got a demo tape and nobody wants to hear it. But it's like this: the South got something to say, and that's all I got to say."

Andre 3000's statement is reminiscent of discourses heard more recently in the context of French rap. In 2013, the group Psy 4 de la Rime was interviewed in a show on YouTube focused on the following topic: "Is it necessary to move to Paris to succeed?" (wwwlillouxcom, 2013). Originally from Marseille, this group had been at the forefront of French rap throughout the 2000s before some of its members undertook successful solo careers. Yet, one of the rappers, Alonzo, declared, "You have to work 3 times, even 4 times more when you come from outside of Paris ... When an artist from outside of Paris is buzzing, it is hard to climb up. So, you need to be 3 times, more creative, more aggressive, more willing to succeed."[1]

This declaration raises questions: while the Outkast statement had been performative, announcing the rise of Southern artists that would soon dominate US music charts, why have these geographical hierarchies remained prevalent in a country 15 times smaller than the US, and with a population of only one fifth? Moreover, what made these inequalities last in a decade marked by the rise of virtual platforms, an evolution that has been announced as leading to the end of "hip-hop regionalism" (Weiner, 2012)?

To answer these questions, it is necessary to examine the distinctive role local scenes have played over time in the French and American rap industries. This chapter will demonstrate that rap offers a viable case study for the analysis of spatial hierarchies that have structured the music industry in both countries, how artists deal with them, and how they have been reconfigured in the "digital context" (Hracs et al., 2016).

By the idea of spatial hierarchies, I refer in this chapter to the existence of inequalities and the importance that various local contexts occupy in the practice of music. These hierarchies are highlighted, for example, when observing the unequal visibility of local scenes within music sales on a national level, or differences in the amount of resources available for artists in various cities. These hierarchies result in cities being associated with different "scales" of music practices: while some are just considered as "local" scenes, others (e.g., artistic capitals) often become synonymous with the "national" and "global" music industry (Guibert, 2006). In this chapter, I consider how these spatial hierarchies constraint artists' careers—as they lead to barriers among scenes that restrict access to crucial music networks—but also to what extent artists can contribute to the "rescaling" (Brenner, 2001) of their local scene, by changing its image and helping it move from the margin to the center of the music industry.

The rap music genre provides a particularly suitable genre to highlight these hierarchies. Since its birth almost 50 years ago, rap has acquired a major role, both in the US (Hess, 2010) and globally (Mitchell, 2001). Yet, the rooting in local and regional spaces has remained a central dimension in the genre, and a defining element of the artists' perceived

[1] In this chapter, all translations from French to English are by the author.

authenticity: many rappers have claimed to "represent" specific regions and cities (Forman, 2002) and they have often been interviewed as spokespersons of specific urban neighborhoods (Hammou, 2012). Through their performances, rappers have shed light on peripheral locations in the music industry, but this visibility has been uneven. In the US especially, the history of rap has been linked to struggles to put new regions on the rap map, first the West Coast in the 1980s (Forman, 2002), and then the South in the early 2000s (Miller, 2008).

This chapter focuses on two urban areas—Lille (France) and Atlanta (United States)—and observe the evolution of their respective roles in French and American rap from 2000 to 2015. While the geography of rap has often been analyzed through its expansion in the 1990s and 2000s (Forman, 2002; Hammou, 2012), the 2000–2015 period shows the genre entering a deep reconfiguration. While rap had become a well-established genre in France and the US, it took place in the context of a music market in crisis, due to the rise of virtual platforms in music consumption (e.g., online streaming and downloading) and production and mediation (e.g., online promotion and communication on social networks) (Leyshon, 2014). Therefore, this case study provides an opportunity to analyze to what extent this evolving context contributed to reshape the hierarchies that had long structured the music industry.

This chapter proceeds in several steps. After introducing my theoretical and methodological approach, I give an overview of the spatial hierarchies that structure the French and US rap maps. Then I explore how these hierarchies have gradually evolved on two levels: changes in the image of these local scenes, and in the artists' promotional strategies. I show that, despite having a similar position originally in the genre, Atlanta and Lille have followed very different trajectories, revealing distinctive power relations in French and American music industries, but also their reconfiguration over time.

2   Situating Local Scenes: Bridging the Gap Between the Geography of Creative Economy and the Social Analysis of Popular Music Genres

The study conducted in this chapter connects two types of analyses involving the distribution of the music industry's infrastructures, mainly formulated in economic geography, and local music scenes, linked to popular music studies. While these analyses have often been developed separately, they provide complementary perspectives to recognize the spatial hierarchies structuring the music industries.

Since the 1990s, research in Anglophone geography has highlighted the existence of significant spatial dimensions surrounding the practice of music (Leyshon et al., 1995; Connell & Gibson, 2002; Johansson & Bell, 2009). While most work focused on the role of music in the representation, practices, or development of spaces and places, some also highlighted how music structures distinctive professional worlds. These studies, carried out by economic geographers, often focused on the distribution of the music industry's infrastructures on a national level. In the US, Scott (1999) analyzed how the distribution of recording companies at the end of the 1990s bore an "uneven relationship to the underlying geography of population" (p. 1970), with a pattern dominated by three agglomerations—Los Angeles, New York, and Nashville. Scott highlighted how, in these cities, a more supportive environment led local artists to be over-represented in music charts. Despite the reconfiguration of the industry in the 2000s, this pattern has hardly changed and, in a more recent study, Florida and Jackson (2010) ended up with similar results. The Martin Prosperity Institute's research team even hypothesized that, paradoxically, the digital shift in music production and consumption had reinforced agglomeration effects which works in favor of the main music centers, leading to the development of new "pop/entertainment complexes" (Florida, 2013).

Similarly, in France, research has highlighted how the geography of the music industry is very centralized and it shows an unchallenged domination of the Parisian region. In France, a long history of state policies and private initiatives has led to a strong domination of Paris over the rest of the country, which can be felt on political, economic, but also cultural levels. While hosting a unique concentration of large-scale cultural facilities, Paris is also a "center of gravity for artistic consumption" as practices in this domain are not only more important but also distinct compared to the rest of the country (Menger, 1993). The specific role of Paris can also be felt in the music industry. In the early 2000s, Calenge (2002) observed that one third of the studios and half of the record labels' offices—including all the major labels—were located in the Paris and its suburbs. He concluded that the French music industry was actually a "regional system of production located in the Parisian agglomeration" (p. 48). The sociologist Gérôme Guibert (2006) highlighted how this situation is the result of a long history: since Paris has been the place of birth of the French music industry in the 1920s, it has become the city where most of the private investment regarding music is concentrated. This structure has remained steady throughout the twentieth and twenty-first century, despite the development of local scenes in the rest of France since the 1980s, following a wave a proactive public policies.[2]

While these works on the music economy are particularly useful to identify the spatial hierarchies that structure national music industries, they don't say much about how artists navigate this economic system, and how their geographical origin might create opportunities or barriers for their careers. These elements have been approached in a second type of study, carried out by popular music scholars.

From the 1980s onward, popular music studies has emerged as an interdisciplinary field that aims to study music genres developed in an industrialized context (Shuker, 2005). This field experienced a "geographical turn" (Straw quoted in Janotti Jr., 2012) in the 1990s, thanks to a new perspective addressing the importance of "local scenes." Originally used loosely by musicians and fans (Cohen, 1999), the scenes idea has been approached in various ways by researchers. Following Straw (1991), some researchers imagine a local scene as a "cultural space in which a range of musical practices coexist" (p. 373). Conversely, Bennett and Peterson (2004) insisted on the distinction between the local scene and the external world. They defined scenes as "the contexts in which clusters of producers, musicians, and fans collectively share their common musical tastes and collectively distinguish themselves from others" (p. 1). However, both perspectives agreed on the idea that the scene is a localized artistic world in which the practice of music is rooted, which is sustained by the presence of key actors and infrastructures, and which can potentially become associated with a coherent "sound" thanks to the exportation of local artists and songs (Grassy, 2010).

Contrary to the literature in the economic geography of music, this body of work has often overlooked the articulation between practices taking place in local scenes or the ones taking place in other spaces or levels. Indeed, most analyses have been limited to highlighting the relation between local practices and "global" music trends (Straw, 1991; Harris,

---

[2] While this chapter focuses on French and US cases, this economic geography of music has also been explored elsewhere, with works on the UK (Watson, 2008) and on Swedish artists in global music networks (Johansson, 2020).

2000; Elafros, 2013), or observing the existence of wider "translocal" scenes (Bennett & Peterson, 2004).[3]

However, while economic geographers only focused on the location of music infrastructures, popular music scholars have highlighted how the structure of local scenes is tied to the expression of specific values. This dimension has linked local scenes to another body of work that brings "authenticity" to the foreground. In popular music, some songs and artists are often evaluated as being more "real" than others (Barker & Taylor, 2007). The attribution of this authenticity is always a construction, which stems from an authentication process (Moore, 2002) undertaken by both audiences and music industry stakeholders (Peterson, 1997). This attribution is influenced by location; in many genres, the "authenticity" of artists is linked to the expression of a rooting in place, whether rural (Peterson, 1997) or urban (Forman, 2002). Authentication can also be influenced by the geography of music production: in the US, many local scenes have gained credibility in specific genres as they emerged as important centers of productions, whether in blues (Chicago), country (Nashville), or soul music (Detroit and Memphis) (Grassy, 2010).

Local scenes have long been crucial arenas for the debates on music genres' authenticity (Shank, 1994; Harkness, 2011; Ondrej & Koubek, 2012; Elafros, 2013). However, the rise of new tools of communication has led to speculations on whether the role of these spaces would start to fade. In the context of rap music, the question of the relation between new internet-based spaces and traditional local artistic contexts has led to particularly intense debates. For the journalist Jonah Weiner (2012), this digital shift would lead to a decrease in the significance in the localized scenes and expressions that were once central to rap music, as the genre would be increasingly produced and consumed on online networks and streaming platforms. Conversely, Sigler and Balaji (2013) have noticed that new generations of rappers continue to "represent" their hometowns, but they argue that this practice is just the result of a commodification process, as labels still utilize this idea as part of the rappers' branding strategies.

I contend, however, that this role of local discourses and music scenes should be understood in relation to the various spaces among which rappers navigate their careers. From 2000 to 2015, these are the artistic capitals—which hosts the main infrastructures of the national music

---

[3] There are a few exceptions to this. See, for example, Ballico (2013).

industry—but also new platforms gradually emerging in the virtual sphere. In relation to this evolving music economy, artists negotiate their local affiliations depending on how their scene is perceived in the temporal and spatial context in which they operate.

3   STUDYING LOCAL SCENES: A LOCAL AND NATIONAL ANALYSIS OF RAP MUSIC ECONOMIES

This paper provides a comparative analysis of France and the US, with the idea that it provides a fruitful perspective to highlight the specificities of their music economies, and their evolution over time. As the place of origin of rap, the US is a country where rap has a significant role in listening practices and consumption. Between 1999 and 2008, rap/hip-hop was the second or third top-selling genre in the country (RIAA, 2008) and, associated with R&B, it ranked second after rock in sales in 2014 (Nielsen, 2014). France's significance in rap was recognized early, with many journalists and scholars regularly promoting it as global rap's second nation (Krims, 2002). While the importance of rap in music listening has long been hard to identify—rap albums were frequently downloaded illegally in the 2000s—the inclusion of streaming in music charts in 2016 has revealed rap as the most listened-to music genre in the country. This evolution also underlined the importance of virtual platforms for rap's consumption as, in 2018, the genre composed 65% of the music listened to on streaming platforms, while it counted for only 43% of the gold certified albums (Mouv', 2018).

In this context, comparing France and the US focuses on two robust rap economies. Yet, this comparison raises the risk of equating quite different countries in terms of their area, population, and size of their music industry.[4] For this reason, the analysis focuses on more similar entities: local scenes.

The urban regions of Lille and Atlanta each constitute "intermediate" cases in the wider national rap industry. Indeed, they are both located outside the historical centers of rap music in respective country, which has contributed to their artists' struggle. Yet, they are scenes with long histories: a first wave of rappers emerged in Atlanta as early as the 1980s (Miller, 2008), and at least a dozen groups operated in the Lille region in the early

---

[4] Between 2001 and 2013, the revenues of the US music market are between five or seven times bigger than the French market (Source: IFPI).

1990s (Cissé, 1992). Moreover, both cities have progressively emerged as regional hotbeds for the practice of rap. In the 2000s, Atlanta came at the forefront of a new Southern rap subgenre, the "Dirty South," which filled the US music charts (Miller, 2008). While Lille has not been as important, it has served as a center that artists from the region attempt to occupy before seeking national success.

Despite these common points, each scene has followed a different path. In this chapter, I will highlight this evolution thanks to data collected through several methodologies: a cartography of rap music sales on the national scale from 2001 to 2012, a documentary analysis of the main music productions in each scene during the same period, and ethnographic fieldwork (based on observations and 40 interviews) on the strategies of local artists during the first half of the 2010s. Whereas the two first methods will provide some insights to the transformations which affected French and American rap music until the beginning of the 2010s, the third method explores how they have changed in the subsequent years of the study.

4   Setting the Scene(s): Mapping the Dominant Imaginary of French and American Rap Music

From 2000 to 2012, French and American rappers operated in a national rap music environment where some locations have more visibility than others (Hess, 2010). This hierarchy is crucial since, as in several other popular music genres, the cartography of the most visible scenes forms a dominant geographical imaginary according to which the authenticity of artists is evaluated (Grassy, 2010). In order to understand Lille and Atlanta's trajectories, it is important to first identify this dominant rap map in the French and American music industries.

French (2015) provided insights to these cores and peripheries in national rap. However, this analysis remained limited to American rappers mentioned on Wikipedia, where the existence of a profile is not linked to a clear threshold in sales or notoriety. I adopted another criterion—the albums that reached gold sales certification. Used both in France and in the US, this certification offers a good comparison by highlighting the artists which have been the most successful in each country.

Using this criterion for the 2000s raises two issues. First, the organizations in charge of their attribution, the Recording Industry Association of

America (RIAA) in the US, and the Syndicat National de l'Edition Phonographique (SNEP) in France, do not provide any classification in terms of genre. Therefore, the research database was built manually, using as a reference the albums which included a majority of rapped lyrics in at least half of the tracks. The second issue is linked to the certifications' threshold. Facing a market in crisis, each organization adopted distinct strategies: whereas the RIAA maintained the same threshold for gold record status (500,000 albums), the SNEP changed it to maintain its symbolic status: originally fixed at 100,000 albums, it was changed to 75,000 in 2006 and to 50,000 in 2009. Nevertheless, in this study, I am not interested in studying this certification simply as a quantitative criterion, but as a qualitative one: in each music industry, a gold album continued to signify success, and artists continued to promote it as a symbol of their role in rap.

Once the list was established, each album was associated with a spatial location. Due to the focus on the visibility of local scenes, the identification of location was based on the geographical origin claimed by the artists rather than the place of production of the album. In rap music, such locations are easy to identify as artists "represent" a hometown in music tracks or interviews (Forman, 2002). This area generally corresponds to a place that has been important to the artists' trajectory (whether as a place of birth, place of residence, or the location where they started their career). While the type of location represented can vary in terms of scales, depending on the artist (it can be a neighborhood, a town, a region), it often remains steady throughout the career, and its display has particular significance as it is often heralded as an element of the artists' authenticity (Forman, 2002).

For the list of gold certified albums, I primarily used the location represented by artists in their music lyrics, as it is the main medium through which artists are associating themselves with specific places. This method allowed me to link most artists of the corpus with a specific location, although it left a few cases where origin remained unclear. In these cases, I looked for a mention of a geographical origin in specialized media (such as interviews in blogs and mentions in the rap lyrics depository Genius), on the basis that these mediums would display a location that artists and their management would agree being associated with, whether voluntarily (by promoting it in their official bio) or tacitly (by not contradicting an assertion made by journalists or commentators). As these locations could be linked to various geographical scales, I made the choice to aggregate them into metropolitan areas for the US, and the *departement*—a French territorial division equivalent to a county—for France. Figures 5.1 and 5.2 show the maps produced through this process, indicating a distinct pattern in each country.

In the US, the maps show a polycentric system. This hierarchy correlates with the demographic distribution in the country—with an absence of albums in the central areas and a significant number in the North East, West or South—and its urban hierarchy. Out of the ten main rap centers during the whole period, five came from the ten most populated metropolitan areas of the country.

These maps also highlight specific patterns and dynamics. In the first half of the 2000s, the rap map is dominated by one city—New York (53 albums)—followed by other cities on the West Coast and in the South. This pattern is the result of a recent evolution; if, in the 1990s, the geography of the genre was mainly associated with the East and West coasts (Forman, 2002), this situation changed by the early 2000s with the rise of Southern artists. Roni Sarig notes that, in 2002, more than 50% of top hip-hop singles in the Billboard music sales and airplay charts involved artists, labels, and producers coming from this region. Therefore, while Atlanta was previously at the margins of American rap, it emerged, in the first half of the 2000s, as the second city on the US map (20 albums), ahead of Los Angeles, despite its population being almost three times smaller.[5]

During this period, Atlanta remains second only to New York. This situation changes between 2006 and 2012. The music industry crisis resulted in a global decrease in the number of certified albums, especially in the former rap capital, leading to a flattening of the hierarchies. Nonetheless, several scenes muddle through the situation. This is the case of many small and mid-size cities, but also of Atlanta which improved its rank: it ascended to the first place (10 albums), surpassing both New York (9 albums) and Los Angeles (7 albums) in the number of certified gold rap recordings.

In France, the rap map shows a different pattern (Fig. 5.2). It illustrates the domination of one central location, the Paris area, which sprawls over eight *departements*. This difference can be explained partly by the smaller

---

[5] From 2000 to 2010, the population of the Metropolitan Statistical Area of Atlanta increased from 4.2 to 5.2 million people, while the one of L.A. rose from 12.3 to 12.8 million (Source: US Census Bureau).

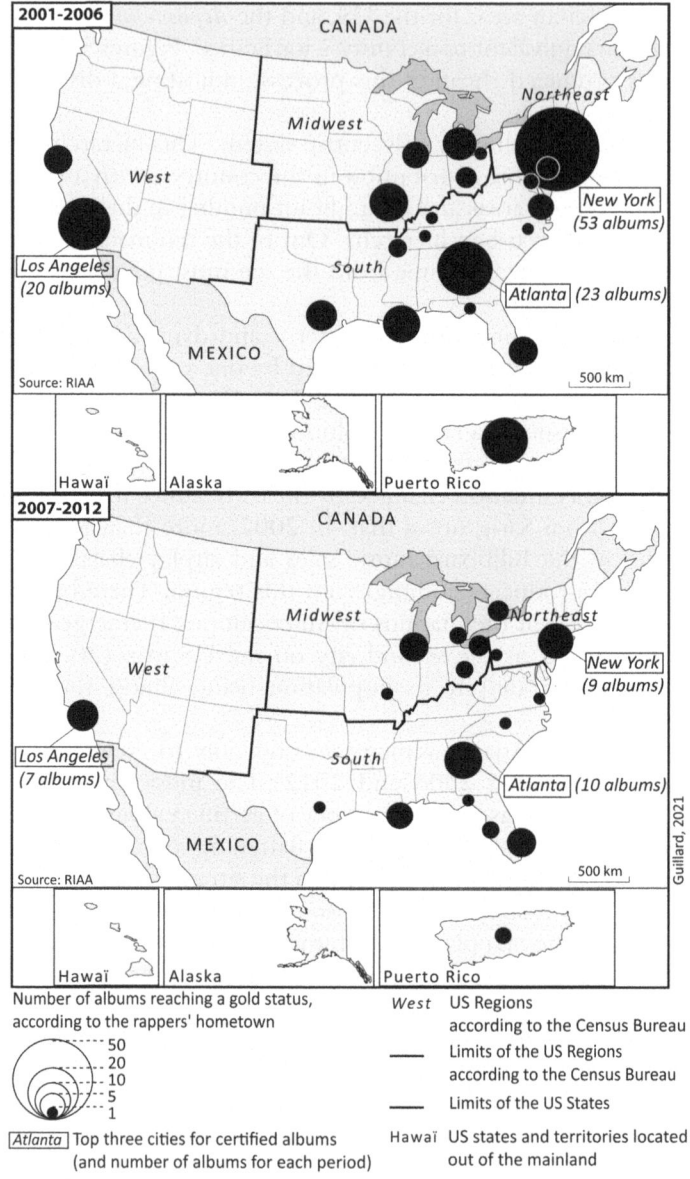

Fig. 5.1   Gold certified albums in US rap music (2001–2012)

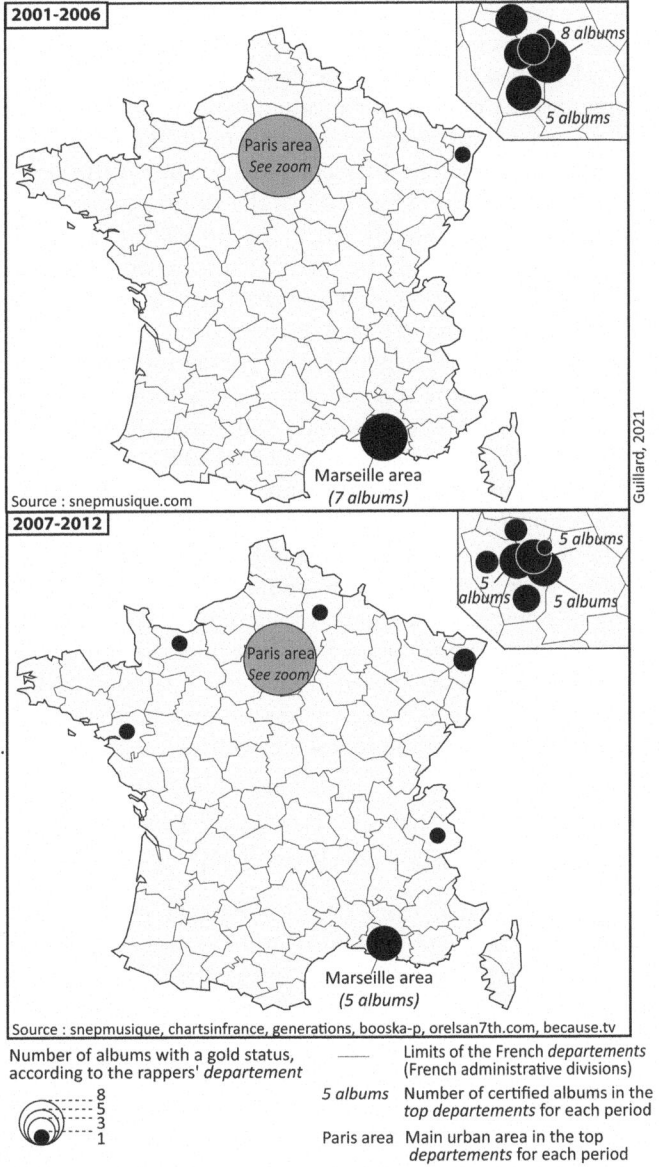

Fig. 5.2 Gold certified albums in French rap music (2001–2012)

size of the country and the population, which does not leave much room for secondary scenes to emerge, and partly by the national urban hierarchy, which is marked by a primacy of the Parisian region.[6]

However, this distribution shows an uneven relation to the country's demography. Two urbans areas are over-represented: the Paris area (three quarters of the albums), and the Marseille area, included in the *departement* of the *Bouches-du-Rhône* (15 to 20% of the albums). Contrary to the US, this situation has been steady since the arrival of rap in France. Throughout the 1990s, almost all the certified albums in French rap were released by artists claiming a hometown in the Paris or Marseille regions, whereas the rest of the country remains blank.

Nevertheless, there is a noticeable change pertaining to the success of albums from other areas in the second half of the 2000s. While only one certified album was released from outside the Paris-Marseille axis from 2001 to 2006, this is the case of six albums from 2007 to 2012. Yet, during this evolution, Lille remains unrepresented in this cartography.

Therefore, in a context of a deep reconfiguration of the polarities of French and American rap, Atlanta and Lille follow opposite trajectories. Even though they were both nationally peripheral in the 1990s, Atlanta emerged as US rap's new center, whereas Lille remained at the margins of French rap, despite a diversification of the rap music centers over time. While echoing long-term hierarchies in French and American music industries, this situation also reflects more or less successful strategies among local artists, as I will explore in the following sections.

5   Putting the City on the Map: Performing the Image of the Scene in Rap Music Recordings

Throughout the 2000s, artists from Lille and Atlanta attempted to build an image of their scene that had credibility in the national music industry. Albums, songs, and related music videos are crucial in this process. As products broadcast to audiences, these media forms collectively convey a discourse that can have a wide impact. Therefore, they play a double role; not only do they reflect the scenes' relative position within each respective national music industry, but they are also the site of performative

[6] In 2011, the urban area of Paris was home to 12.3 million residents, which is significantly higher than the cities ranked second (Lyon 2.2 million) and third (Marseille 1.7 million). The urban area of Lille was the 6th most populated, with 1.2 million (Source: INSEE).

strategies (Austin, 1979) in an effort to inscribe themselves on the rap music map.

Due to the distinct trajectories of Atlanta and Lille, the corpus has not been determined in the same way. In Atlanta, the albums included are the ones which reached a gold record status, based on the database analyzed in the previous section. In Lille, where no artists reached such commercial success, the albums could not be chosen in the same way. Therefore, the corpus was composed of albums consensually deemed as relevant by the scene's members during my fieldwork, because they had reached a certain number of sales, became highly influential in the local scene, or highlighted as particularly representative of the type of rap being produced locally.[7] The goal of this selection process was, in the absence of any artist with a significant commercial success, to put the focus on key figures that could illustrate how the urban region has been represented in the local scene, and how this representation evolved over time. Therefore, if the corpuses for Atlanta and Lille include very different types of albums—if we compare their production budget or their commercial impact—these data sets are particularly interesting to compare, as they reflect the specific ways of representing the city that have emerged in each local scene, and how rappers have attempted to situate them in the broader contexts of French and American rap music. In total, the corpus is composed of 33 albums in Atlanta and 40 in Lille, released between 2001 and 2012.

This does not mean that Atlanta and Lille albums are produced with the same budget, or that they have the same impact on rap music nationally. Moreover, Atlanta only features artists that have had mainstream success, while Lille data also include less-known artists.

In both cases, the representation of each city changed over time, although in different ways. In Atlanta, four main steps can be noticed. First, in the early 2000s, rappers from Atlanta had to deal with a city that was not associated with a distinct image in US rap, and many tracks attempted to present the city to a broader audience. A prime example is the music video *Welcome to Atlanta*, released by Jermaine Dupri and Ludacris. At the time of its release, in 2001, Jermaine Dupri was already an important figure of the local rap industry. Active as a producer since

---

[7] In addition to cross-checking the names of groups and albums mentioned during the interviews, the composition of this corpus was based on extensive conversation with a few key actors, whose long trajectory and central role in the scene (e.g., as a radio DJ or studio owner) allowed them to collect a significant number of local records.

1991, he founded the record label So So Def in 1993, to which he signed the first generation of Atlanta rap and R&B artists that experienced national success.[8] In Dupri's words, the idea of *Welcome to Atlanta* was to release a "theme song" which can "welcome people in our city" (Sarig, 2007, p. 189). This intention is illustrated in the clip that depicts Dupri and fellow Atlantan Ludacris guiding tourists through the city on a bus, in an obvious parody of tour operator companies. The video draws a parallel between the rappers' function and that of a tour guide, each with the aim to present the city to outsiders. The video features several iconic Atlanta sites, represented through maps, visits of the main neighborhoods, or images of famous landmarks (such as Atlanta's main entertainment venue at the time, Phillips Arena). They also present the local rap scene: the front of the tour bus displays the words "Dirty South," which refers to the new wave of rappers from the region and the guided tour is labeled as "crunk," referring to a local subgenre emerging at the time.

A few years later, the representation of the scene had changed. The success of several rappers led Atlanta to become a new center of US rap, but the city's rise was not well received by the genre's ostensible gatekeepers. In 2006, New York's veteran rapper Nas released an album called *Hip-Hop is Dead*, that many Southern rappers perceived as a charge against their newfound influence in the genre. In this second period, many tracks show the need for proving the city's authenticity compared to more established rap capitals. One example is *Help is Coming*, a track released by T.I. in 2007, where the rapper asserts, "To the fans and the critics / Think hip-hop is missing / This is a lil' proof that hip-hop livin' /…in the ATL, see hip-hop chillin' / In a multimillion dollar crib hip-hop building" (T.I., 2007).

In a third step, this sense of belonging to Atlanta starts to fade, as several artists that initially represented the city and the region showed a willingness to expand their affiliations: Ludacris asserts "I'm universal, Luda never limits himself to the South" (*War on God* on *Ludacris*, 2006) while T.I. claims that he "went from the King of the South to the King of States" (*Raw* on *T.I.*, 2007). If this change can be associated with individual careers—Ludacris and T.I. evolving from Southern artists to well-established national rappers—it also reflects broader transformations in the image of Atlanta and the South. While the phrase "Dirty South" was widely used in the early 2000s, it progressively disappears afterwards, a

---

[8] On his label at the time were Kriss Kross, Da Brat, and TLC.

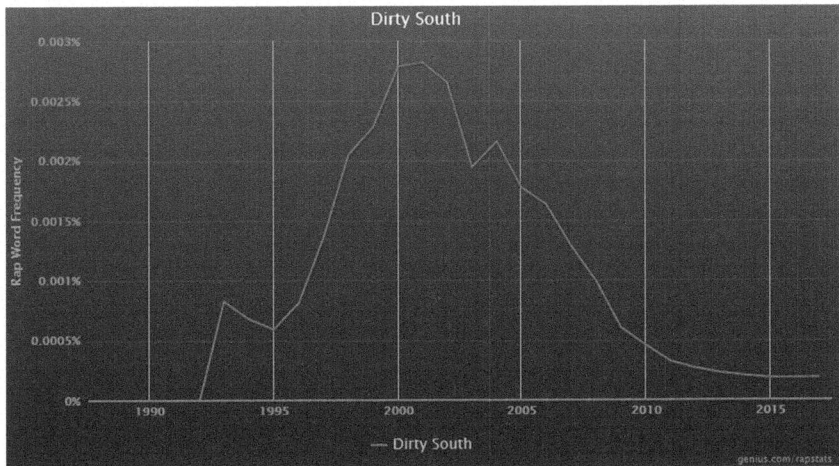

Fig. 5.3 Word frequency of the term "Dirty South" in rap lyrics available on Rap Genius. Source: https://genius.com/rapstats. Generated on February 6, 2021

decrease that can be discerned on the online rap lyrics site Rap Genius (Fig. 5.3). The authenticity constructions of Southern rap reflect an evolution of its role in the music industry, whereby it shifts from a marginalized subgenre to the US rap's new standard.

Yet, the image of Atlanta also experienced a rebirth in the early 2010s, with a new generation of artists representing the city differently. This is illustrated by B.o.B.'s first album, *The Adventures of Bobby Ray* (B.o.B., 2010). Before experiencing massive success, this rapper started his career in Atlanta's local scene. A turning point occurred when he was noticed by an executive from Atlantic Records in a local open-mic session, at a time when these events were career launchpads for local artists (Guillard, 2014). Therefore, in his song *Airplanes Part 2*, Atlanta is not mentioned as a city but as a scene where rappers are trying to build a career ("Trying to be the next rapper coming out the A (A-Town) / Hoping for a record deal to ignore my pain"). Here again, the representation conveyed in local artists' lyrics echoes an evolution of Atlanta, from an unknown space to a new hotbed of the rap industry.

Conversely, in Lille, the representation of the city underwent different changes. Even as this urban region has hosted a dynamic scene since the 1980s, it still sat at the margins of French rap in the early 2000s. Tracks produced during this period echo this situation. Among them is *La Malediction du 5-9*, a song produced by the group Juste Cause on an album released in 2001, which refers to a curse ("*malédiction*") which would touch the 59th *département* of France (the North) which comprises Lille's urban area. They rap, "In short we are a number of talented people who / Weren't lucky enough to live in Marseille or Paris / ... We buried our dreams of gold records, gold mics / The gold seekers will not dare to explore this place / It is a minefield and the roads are blocked with stones" (Juste Cause, 2001).

While claiming that their local scene is not recognized on a national scale, this song is also a performative way to construct a visibility for Lille and its region in rap imaginaries. During the second half of the twentieth century, the North of France became one of France's main mining regions, leading waves of migrants to move into the area to work in the booming coal industry. In this track, the rappers use references to the mines as metaphors for the region's role in the rap industry. They present the region as a "minefield," conveying the double meaning of an area where the main label's executive will not dare to come, even though it is full of "gold nuggets."

This attempt to put Lille on the rap map developed further in the following years. In the mid-2000s, several local artists started to experience recognition beyond the local scene. These opportunities are indicative of a new visibility. This is expressed by the group Les Amateurs, who signed a record deal with Sony during this period. Following their contract, they released a music video titled *5-9 sous les flashs* (5-9 under the spotlights) in which they assert: "5-9, we are here to match your Paris-Marseille!" (Les Amateurs, 2006). The video is filmed in one of the city's main housing projects, in the local subway, and features several rappers from the local and regional scene. However, while in Atlanta the discourse of local rappers changed along with city's increasing recognition, the same process did not happen in the North of France. The story of Les Amateurs illustrates this situation: after their first mixtape, the group did not release an album as expected, leading to the end of their record deal and a gap of several years in their career.

Because of this, the city was still not associated with a distinct image in French rap at the end of the decade. This led to a stagnation in the way the city is represented, sometimes accompanied by some resentment. Within a collaborative track released in 2009, the rapper Saknes asserts: "Lille! So many wasted songs, wasted talents, we got angry, gave up / On our ambitions because year after year nothing happens along the way" (Axiom, 2009).

Therefore, throughout the 2000s, the performances carried out in Lille and Atlanta do not have the same success. In Atlanta, musical releases reflect, and even anticipate, the trajectory of a scene which becomes a new rap capital in the US. In Lille, local rappers are not as successful, leading to a stagnation in the geographical imaginaries. However, we can't understand these evolutions if we only look at the content of the rap songs, as the impact of songs is strongly correlated with the success that artists have been able to achieve. On this level, as I will explain in the remaining section, the scenes of Atlanta and Lille have supported their local artists' strategies in different ways.

6 MAKING A WAY OUT OF THE SCENE: THE ROLE OF LOCAL RESOURCES IN THE ARTISTS' CAREER

While being represented in songs and videos, the scenes of Lille and Atlanta are also physical areas inhabited by rappers. In popular music, artists build their career through commitments to several spaces of practice, which help them to build a "buzz" (Johansson, 2020) and move from the local scene to the national scale.

From the 2000s to the 2010s, artists from Lille and Atlanta did not navigate the industry in the same ways. On this level, we can notice the existence of circular effects between practices and representations; while the artists' strategies influenced the evolution of the scenes' image throughout the 2000s, they were in turn influenced by an already established image of these spaces, which is more or less advantageous for their career. In the first half of the 2010s, the rise of enhanced virtual platforms reinforced this dichotomy as artists used them differently.

6.1 Atlanta: Leveraging the Local Scene for National Recognition

From the end of the 2000s to the beginning of the 2010s, Atlanta appears particularly well-suited for mobilizing an artist's career. This is partly the result of the city's musical history. While Atlanta has long held a secondary musical reputation compared to other Southern cities (e.g., New Orleans or Memphis), it wasn't completely marginalized. In the 1960s and 1970s, many studios opened in the city, which transformed it into a significant hub for soul and funk music (Tullos et al., 2003). Rap music benefited from this legacy, and several rap studios moved into already existing spaces. In the 2000s, the success of local rappers reinforced this existing music economy, as Atlanta became a speculative bubble, with major labels scouring the city in search of the next rap star.

During the field research, Atlanta was described as a place where artists can find support from early career to mainstream success. For artists starting in rap music, Atlanta is a good place of practice, as the bar of entry in the local scene is low. A local rapper mentions, "There is no reason not to be a musician here. There are so many studios specialized in rap. So if you wanna be a rapper, you can actually easily find someone to record your music and get it on CDs" (Interview, March 29, 2013).

Atlanta is also good for artist exposure, as the city hosts a number of significant industry-oriented events. An emerging local rapper declares, "There are big conferences happening every year where you can register and meet some people. I think if you are serious with your career, some people in town have to be able to recognize your face" (Interview, October 20, 2013).

At this stage, the difficulty for artists is how to distinguish themselves from others in order to get a record label contract. However, even after a contract is signed, the local scene is still a resource to leverage. In his dissertation, Murali Balaji (2009) showed that Atlanta has a central role in the development strategies of artists signed by major labels. In a first step, Atlanta is used as a testing ground: while helping rappers to gain a first audience, leveraging the local scene is also a way to build the rappers' authenticity, thanks to the recognition by local gatekeepers (mainly radio and club DJs) who have a voice in the music industry. This experience in Atlanta is also an advantage when the promotion reaches a national level. At this point, the city becomes a brand signifier, proving the rappers' authenticity.

During the first half of the 2010s, the increasingly important role of virtual platforms did not fundamentally change this pattern. For some artists, it became a way to complement the leveraging of the local scene, in order to strengthen the relations that they had already established in physical space. For others, it was a way to challenge aesthetic norms that had become too rigid over time. Indeed, the success of Atlanta rap had a notable side effect. In interviews, several artists mentioned that, due to their association with the city, they often faced expectations from the industry regarding their sound or image. As an A&R representative at Atlantic

Records explained, leveraging the resources provided by virtual platforms offers a way to bypass these expectations: "As an Atlanta artist, I think if you are not doing a certain type of music, it will be hard to get radio play, to get in the clubs, to get labels interested in you. So you have to take it on yourself to use the internet … to build a buzz. Then it will trickle down to the clubs, and then the radios will play it" (Interview, February 20, 2013).

Observations in local shows confirm this statement. At this period, it was common to hear artists announcing the number of views that their videos had generated on YouTube before their performance in open mics, emphasizing a significant online "buzz" as an illustration of their success to come. The achievement of specific milestone on this level (e.g., the threshold of 1 million views) was also frequently promoted in the local scene, for example by organizing a celebration party. Therefore, in this case, the role of the local music scene is not fading. The internet is used first and foremost as a means to reach local infrastructures. Success on online platform has become a token aimed at local gatekeepers, signifying that they already have a "movement" that could help them to reach wider success.

6.2 Lille: Bypassing the Local and Shattering the National "Glass Ceiling"

In Lille, the difficulties of local rappers reflect a strong disconnect between the local scene and the national industry. Lille hosts an important number of music venues but, until 2015, they were not seen as a way to help the rappers' development. Firstly, most of them are publicly funded, an outcome of state investment policies toward local music scenes in the 1980s and 1990s (Guibert, 2006). Even though these venues helped with the recognition of artists located outside Paris, they remained peripheral in an industry still dominated by the French capital. Secondly, in the 1980s and 1990s, these venues were taken over mainly by activists from punk and rock scenes; and, in the early 2010s, they still focused on those genres. In 2013, a study focused on the North *departement* showed that "Rap, hip-hop and reggae" comprised less than 5% of the shows programmed in these venues (CNV, 2014).

Therefore, throughout the 2000s, the rappers' strategies were based on the idea of escaping the local scene. They adopted several tactics to this end, but most of them hit a "glass ceiling," due to the lack of knowledge of the music industry's norms and networks. The trajectory of the group Les Amateurs illustrates this situation. After having started in the local scene at the end of the 1990s, the group participated in a talent show in 2003 called "Max de 109" (Max of New Blood[9]) organized by the main rap radio station in France, Skyrock, in partnership with Sony Music. They were one of the five winners, which led to an appearance on a compilation album that was distributed nationally. However, this first exposure did not turn into long-term success. A member of the group explains, "It was supposed to lead to a record deal [and] it could lead to a full album if things were going well … But they ended up settling a deal with [another rapper], La Fouine because they could relate more to him" (Interview, April 19, 2014). The choice of La Fouine instead of Les Amateurs is strongly linked to a difference in pre-existing contacts in the music industry. For this rapper from the Parisian region, Max de 109 was a starting point of a very successful career as one of the main figures of French rap. In his autobiography, he recalls that he heard about the contest through his manager:

> Clément [his manager] called me to tell me that … the executives from Sony … wanted to settle a record deal with me, and they wanted me to register to evaluate the impact of my upcoming album … In the label's office, I understood that I wasn't dreaming … The executives were talking to me like: "You are the French Snoop Dogg, you sing, and we are going to take care of you" … I won the contest, far ahead of the others … For Sony, it was in the bag, and they did what they had to do. (La Fouine et al., 2013, pp. 213–214)

In this regard, the experience of Les Amateurs from the scene of Lille was not only useless to the group, it also placed them at a disadvantage compared to a Parisian artist who was already at the heart of national music industry.

In the 2010s, the rise of virtual platforms offered local artists a way to bypass the local scene's glass ceiling. This is how, after decades of attempts, one artist from the Lille urban area, Gradur, finally gained major success. Originally serving in the army, Gradur was wounded in 2013. During his recovery time, he released rap videos on YouTube. Around the same time, he met a Parisian rapper at a showcase in the North of France, who

---

[9] "109" should be understood here as a numerical abbreviation of "Sang Neuf," pronounced the same way, which is used to refer to a new wave of French rappers.

introduced him to Tonton Marcel, a Parisian blogger who was at this time a key talent scout in the rap world. A few months later, Gradur was interviewed on his YouTube channel. This connection to Parisian networks brought him better exposure and, in early 2014, one of his videos was shared by Booba, a French rap superstar. This made Gradur the new "buzz" of French rap and he signed a deal with a subsidiary of Universal, Barclay, which resulted in an album that reached gold status.

While Les Amateurs were involved in the local scene as a potential stepping stone to the national industry, Gradur used the internet to bypass the local scene in order to reach the Parisian networks more directly. However, this lack of local involvement was criticized among local stakeholders. As a manager and radio host from Lille mentions, "Gradur, for me, he is not really a 'Northern' artist. The proof is, right now, he is buzzing in Paris … without stopping by the region … Because his style is really closer to [Parisian rappers] than what we do here" (Interview, June 20, 2014). Despite bringing exposure to the Lille urban area, Gradur embodies a common fear locally—the idea that virtual platforms might contribute to a loss of the aesthetics which were once specific to the Northern rap scene. Instead of putting the city and the region on the map, these strategies would contribute to erasing these aesthetics by aligning them more closely with national trends.

7   Conclusion

While some authors have announced a gradual erasing of the role of local scenes in the production of rap music due to the rise of virtual platforms, this chapter has showed how, over the past decades, the evolution of the geographical hierarchies structuring French and American rap music has been more complex.

In both France and the US, rappers operate in a music economy marked by strong geographical inequalities. However, this structure varies: the US has a polycentric system, while in France the music industry is centralized in Paris. Far from existing "naturally," these hierarchies are the result of both a long-term history of the music industry and a short-term history of rap. On this level, this chapter showed how the economic geography of music on a national level and the authenticity constructions in local scenes mutually influence each other. Indeed, rather than accepting that their careers will be hindered by their location, artists emerging in local scenes often build performances and strategies which aim to changes national hierarchies, nudging peripheral practices toward the center of the music industry.[10] However, the ability of artists to challenge the dominant structure of the music industry depends on the role that local scenes have in each country, as it is more or less possible for them to be "re-scaled" (Brenner, 2001) as central places in the national music industry. In the US, the Atlanta scene gradually became a new capital of American rap music, echoing a US context where "third cities" have often emerged besides New York and Los Angeles to help to the development of specific music genres. Meanwhile, in France, Lille stayed at the margins of French rap, illustrating the difficulty for local scenes to gain visibility in a centralized industry, and the existence of a spatial "glass ceiling" between local practices and the national music industry based in the French capital. Rather than making these geographical hierarchies disappear, the rise of the internet in artists' practices has added an additional layer to this structure: the local scene, the national music industry, and virtual platforms have become several nodes among which artists navigate to build their career in the rap world.

<h2>References</h2>

Austin, J. L. (1979). Performative utterances. In *Philosophical papers* (3rd ed., pp. 233–252). Clarendon Press.

Balaji, M. (2009). *Trap(ped) music and masculinity: The cultural production of Southern Hip-Hop at the intersection of corporate control and self-construction.* Doctoral thesis, Pennsylvania State University.

Ballico, C. (2013). *Bury me deep in isolation: A cultural examination of a peripheral music industry and scene.* PhD Dissertation, Edith Cowan University.

Barker, H., & Taylor, Y. (2007). *Faking it: The quest for authenticity in popular music.* W.W. Norton & Company.

Bennett, A., & Peterson, R. (2004). *Music scenes. Local, translocal and virtual.* Vanderbilt University Press.

Brenner, N. (2001). The limits to scale? Methodological reflections on scalar structuration. *Progress in Human Geography, 25*(4), 591–614.

Calenge, P. (2002). Les Territoires de l'innovation: les réseaux de l'industrie de la musique en recomposition. *Géographie, Economie, Société, 4*, 37–56.

Cissé, S.-H. (1992). *Rap en Nord.* Miroirs Editions.

[10] While not explored in this chapter, this strategy has to be considered in relation to the existence of an opposite one, which consists of hiding the "local" dimension in favor of national frames, like the one of French 'hoods (Guillard, 2017).

CNV. (2014). *Chiffres de la diffusion des spectacles de musiques actuelles et de variétés. Statistiques commentées et éléments d'évolution 2013–2014.*

Cohen, S. (1999). Scenes. In B. Horner & T. Swiss (Eds.), *Key terms in popular music and culture* (pp. 239–247). Blackwell.

Connell, J., & Gibson, C. (2002). *Sound tracks, popular music, identity and place.* Routledge.

Elafros, A. (2013). Greek hip hop: Local and translocal authentication in the restricted field of production. *Poetics, 41*(1), 75–95.

Florida, R. (2013, May 13). The geography of America's pop music/entertainment complex. *Bloomberg CityLab.* https://www.bloomberg.com/news/articles/2013-05-28/the-geography-of-america-s-pop-music-entertainment-complex

Florida, R., & Jackson, S. (2010). Sonic city: The evolving economic geography of the music industry. *Journal of Planning Education and Research, 29*(3), 310–321.

Forman, M. (2002). *The hood comes first: Race, space and place in rap and hip-hop.* Wesleyan.

French, K. (2015). Geography of American rap: Rap diffusion and rap centers. *Geojournal, 82*(2), 259–272.

Grassy, E. (2010). *Le Lieu musical: du texte à l'espace, un itinéraire sémantique. Poétique des catégories géographiques dans les musiques populaires américaines (1920–2007).* Doctoral dissertation, Université Paris IV Sorbonne.

Guibert, G. (2006). *La production de la culture. Le cas des musiques amplifiées en France.* Irma Editions/Mélanie Séteun.

Guillard, S. (2014). "To be in the place": les *open mics* comme espaces de légitimation dans les scènes rap à Paris et Atlanta. *Belgéo, 4.* https://belgeo.revues.org/13025

Guillard, S. (2017). "Getting the city on lock": imaginaires géographiques et stratégies d'authentification dans le rap en France et aux États-Unis. *L'Information Géographique, 81,* 102–123.

Hammou, K. (2012). *Une Histoire du rap en France.* La Découverte.

Harkness, G. (2011). Backpackers and gangstas: Chicago's white rappers strive for authenticity. *American Behavioral Scientist, 55*(1), 57–85.

Harris, K. (2000). "Roots?" The relationship between the global and the local within extreme metal scene. *Popular Music, 19*(1), 13–30.

Hess, M. (2010). "It's only right to represent where I'm from": Local and regional hip hop scenes in the United States. In M. Hess (Ed.), *Hip-Hop in America: A regional guide. Volume 1: East Coast and West Coast* (pp. vii–xxix). Greenwood Press.

Hracs, B. J., Seman, M., & Virani, T. E. (2016). *The production and consumption of music in the digital age.* Routledge.

Janotti Jr., J. (2012). Interview—Will Straw and the importance of music scenes in music and communication studies. *Revista de Associação National dos Programas de Pos-Graduação, 15*(2). http://www.compos.org.br/seer/index.php/e-compos/article/viewFile/812/599

Johansson, O. (2020). *Songs from Sweden. Shaping pop culture in a globalized music industry*. Palgrave Macmillan.

Johansson, O., & Bell, T. (2009). *Sound, society and the geography of popular music*. Routledge.

Krims, A. (2002). Foreword: Francophone hip-hop as a colonial urban geography. In A.-P. Durand (Ed.), *Black, blanc, beur: Rap music and hip-hop culture in the Francophone world* (pp. vii–x). The Scarecrow Press.

La Fouine, A., Madani, K., & Séranot, C. (2013). *Drôle de parcours*. J'ai lu.

Leyshon, A. (2014). *Reformatted: Code, networks, and the transformation of the music industry*. Oxford University Press.

Leyshon, A., Matless, D., & Revill, G. (1995). The place of music. *Transactions of the Institute of British Geographers, 20*(4), 423–433.

Menger, P.-M. (1993). L'Hégémonie parisienne. Economie et politique de la gravitation artistique. *Annales. Économies, Sociétés, Civilisations, 6*, 1565–1600.

Miller, M. (2008). Dirty decade: Rap music and the U.S. South: 1997–2007. *Southern Spaces*. http://southernspaces.org/2008/dirty-decade-rap-music-and-us-south-1997%E2%80%932007

Mitchell, T. (Ed.). (2001). *Global noise. Rap and hip-hop outside the USA*. Wesleyan University Press.

Moore, A. (2002). Authenticity as authentication. *Popular Music, 21*(2), 209–223.

Mouv'. (2018, July 15). *Baromètre 2018 du Hip Hop en France*. www.irma.asso.fr/Barometre-2018-du-Hip-Hop-en

Nielsen. (2014). *Nielsen music US report*. http://www.nielsen.com/content/dam/corporate/us/en/public%20factsheets/Soundscan/nielsen-2014-year-end-music-report-us.pdf

Ondrej, C., & Koubek, M. (2012). Include 'em all? Culture, politics and a local hardcore/punk scene in the Czech Republic. *Poetics, 40*, 1–21.

Peterson, R. (1997). *Creating country music. Fabricating authenticity*. University of Chicago Press.

RIAA. (2008). *Consumer profile*. http://riaa.com/media/CA052A55-9910-2DAC-925F-27663DCFFFF3.pdf

Sarig, R. (2007). *Third Coast, Outkast, Timbaland and how hip-hop became a Southern thing*. Da Capo Press.

Scott, A.-J. (1999). The US recorded music industry: On the relations between organization, location, and creativity in the cultural economy. *Environment and Planning A, 31*, 1965–1984.

Shank, B. (1994). *Dissonant identities: The rock'n'roll scene in Austin, Texas*. University Press of New England.

Shuker, R. (2005). *Popular music. The key concepts* (2nd ed.). Routledge.
Sigler, T., & Balaji, M. (2013). Regional identity in contemporary hip-hop music: (Re)presenting the notion of place. *Communication, Culture & Critique, 6*, 336–352.
Straw, W. (1991). System of articulation and logic of change: Communities and scenes in popular music. *Cultural Studies, 5*(3), 368–388.
Tullos, A., Miller, M., & Dowd, T. (2003). Atlanta: A city without sound? *Footnotes, Newsletter of the American Sociological Association, 31*(5). http://www.asanet.org/footnotes/mayjun03/indexone.html
Watson, A. (2008). Global music city: Knowledge and geographical proximity in London's recorded music industry. *Area, 40*(1), 12–23.
Weiner, J. (2012, December 20). Where you're from and where you're @. Azealia Banks, A$AP Rocky, TNGHT, and the end of hip-hop regionalism. *Slate.* http://www.slate.com/articles/arts/music_box/2012/06/azealia_banks_a_ap_rocky_tnght_and_the_end_of_hip_hop_regionalism_.html

DISCOGRAPHY AND VIDEOGRAPHY

Axiom (feat 12 MCs from the North of France). (2009, March 5). *Norside.* https://www.youtube.com/watch?v=uIOFvQP1PZc
B.o.B. (2010). *The adventures of Bobby Ray.* Grand Hustle/Rebel Rock/Atlantic.
Juste Cause. (2001). *La Dette de l'Occident.* http://justecause.free.fr/
Les Amateurs. (2006, September 20). 5-9 sous les flashs. https://www.youtube.com/watch?v=-vJubU6v1ik
Ludacris. (2006). *Release therapy.* Disturbing The Peace/Def Jam South.
T.I. (2007). *T.I. vs T.I.P.* Grand Hustle/Asylum/Atlantic.
wwwlillouxcom. (2013, May 13). *Faut-il quitter sa province pour conquérir Paris ? Avec les Psy 4 de la Rime* [Video]. https://www.youtube.com/watch?v=H8dkTzY9cm8

CHAPTER 6

On the Road: Precarious Work and Life in the Live Music Industry

Adam Zendel

Abstract Musicians rely on touring and live performance in order to earn a living. However, little scholarly research examines the working and living conditions of musicians on tour. This paper explores the lived experience of musicians on tour through three cases of working-class musicians. While live performance and touring enable many to survive in the industry, it exposes musicians to new forms of risk and precarity. Touring is immediately precarious due to the dangers of driving and stage work. While the excitement of travel can be alluring, many describe travel as the most exhausting part of touring. Five themes of precariousness shape the lives of these musicians. First, many musicians feel a need to stay on tour both to avoid costs of regular urban life and to cultivate new markets. Second, musicians experience insecurities related to the logistics of booking tours, including finding places to stay overnight and managing cancelations. Third, musicians experience financial insecurity through contingent contracts and unexpected costs on tour. Fourth, traveling includes many

A. Zendel (✉)
University of Toronto, Toronto, ON, Canada
e-mail: adam.zendel@mail.utoronto.ca

119
O. Johansson et al. (eds.), *New Geographies of Music 1*, Geographies
of Media, https://doi.org/10.1007/978-981-99-0757-1_6

challenges related to self-care. Finally, musicians navigate complex and often contradictory forms of socialization on tour. Together, these themes show how touring exposes musicians and crews to specific forms of risks. With live music becoming the largest subsector of the music industry, it is important to understand the lived experience of touring and the vulnerabilities and risks musicians face on tour.

Keywords Touring musicians • Live music • Employment related geographical mobility • Music geography • Cultural economy • Precarious labor

1   INTRODUCTION

The proliferation and ubiquity of online music streaming has profoundly reconfigured the spatial economy of the music industry. The transition from music sold as a physical media to on-demand streaming has resulted in an industry-wide shift toward live music. Of the three main sectors in the music industry, live music is now the largest one, surpassing recording and licensing in total revenues (Wikström, 2014). A general loss of income from recording pressures artists to tour. Unlike work in recording, live performance and touring exposes workers to unique risks and precariousness. On tour, artists' lives become temporally and geographically fragmented (Zendel, 2020). Constant touring leads to increased insecurity in the predictability of the time and place of their work; their wages and revenue; the places they dwell; and how they care for themselves, their fellow tour-mates, and their families. These forms of insecurity manifest at the scale of the body, heightening the need to negotiate everyday life and the self in new ways.

This chapter follows three case studies to consider the lived experience of touring musicians. There are five themes that emerge from these cases that include economic, logistical, and social challenges (see Sect. 3). Taken together, these cases paint a picture of life as a working musician. Their livelihoods are precariously pieced together through tours and live performance. The proliferation of online music streaming, coupled with broader structural changes to the economy has fragmented time and space of music work. Musicians spend more time booking, performing, and traveling away from home, leading to increased precarity and vulnerability.

2   LIVE MUSIC TAKES OVER

A series of technological disruptions and reconfigurations of capital has made live music the largest sector of the music industry, with artists and businesses earning proportionally more from live music than recording or licensing (Prior, 2018; Tschmuck, 2017; Wikström, 2014). In the late 1990s, widespread music piracy collapsed the value of recorded music. Physical album sales plummeted as music piracy became ubiquitous. Rather than develop new business models, the major record labels pursued a legal response to online file sharing by seeking injunctive relief from file sharing platforms and in some cases even suing the end consumer of pirated music (Sinnreich, 2013). This strategy proved costly and ineffective having little effect at reducing piracy or restoring revenue from recorded music. The piracy crisis was first resolved through the establishment of new online music markets such as iTunes, which through the sale of individual songs changed the medium and mode by which people purchase and listen to music. The growth of streaming platforms, such as Spotify, Apple Music, and Pandora "represents a shift in business models from material ownership to a system built on rent" (Prior, 2018, p. 33). Today, the recorded music market is reconstituted as a service where users rent access rather than own music as a discrete material or digital object. Music businesses have re-secured recorded music as a commodity through streaming platforms (Eriksson et al., 2019). Meanwhile, Holt (2010) observes that live music has in fact grown during the decline of other forms of media. This growth is signaled by rising ticket prices for concerts, growing audience sizes, and the deeper integration of live music into other fields such as advertising and digital culture (Holt, 2010). Concurrently, scholars observe how the work of artists has become more independent, entrepreneurial, and riskier (Coulson, 2012; Haynes & Marshall, 2018; Hracs, 2012; Mühlbach & Arora, 2020). Taken as a whole, the impacts of streaming, digitization and their secondary effects are intimately experienced by artists through a general loss of income and an increased pressure to monetize their music through live performance and touring.

Haynes and Marshall (2018) argue that musicians are a barometer of current trends in the gig economy. Musicians are pressured to be entrepreneurial actors. The rise of streaming and loss of record sales occur alongside larger structural changes to the economy, such as the expansion of gig work and rising costs of living (Standing, 2016). The experience of working musicians is adequately captured in the emerging gig economy and precarious labor literatures. Gill and Pratt (2008) describe precariousness as "all forms of insecure, contingent, flexible work—from illegalized, casualized and temporary employment, to homeworking, piecework and freelancing" (p. 3). These employment characteristics are all found in music work, and are amplified by touring. While many cities are actively trying to support local arts and music scenes, many critics suggest that creative city and music city policies accelerate gentrification (Peck, 2007) displacing artists in the process (Catungal et al., 2009; Markusen, 2006). For musicians displaced by gentrification, touring becomes more than an employment strategy, but a way to avoid high urban rents.

Today, most musicians do not rely on income from recording (Marshall, 2013). The industry at all scales is shifting toward live music production (Wikström, 2014). On the one end, many successful recording artists are now subject to the "360 contract" where in addition to monetizing recording and publishing, record companies expand artist contracts to touring and merchandising (Bacache-Beauvallet et al., 2016; Karubian, 2008; Marshall, 2013; Stahl & Meier, 2012). While on the other end, working musicians do not expect income from their recording activities, often forgoing making recordings altogether. For both elite and working-class musicians, live performance is a reliable source of income allowing them to earn income through ticket and merchandise sales. As such, artists increasingly find themselves traveling to earn a living as a professional musician (Gross & Musgrave, 2016).

While streaming music has re-secured the profitability of recorded music, it has atomized work in the music industry by diffusing both opportunity and income. Artists work more independently, shoulder greater risk, and spend more time carrying out entrepreneurial tasks to the detriment of their music creation and personal well-being. These changes make their lives temporally and geographically fragmented. Musicians are increasingly selling the service and spectacle of music rather than the material of music, reconfiguring the labor process of music production toward myriad activities supporting live performance and touring. Touring as a form of work is not new in any sense; musicians have traveled as long as music has been work. However, due to the changing income composition of musical workers, thriving as a professional musician requires extreme employment-related geographical mobility, along with a suite of entrepreneurial skills, such as promotion, accounting, vehicle mechanics, social media, curation, cooking, and more (Zendel, 2020).

While popular culture and industry writing explores the drudgery of touring or valorizes the luxurious conditions of elite artists, there remains little scholarship on the lived experience of working musicians (cf, McKinna, 2014; Novoa, 2012; Ramella, 2018; Zendel, 2020). The extant scholarship explores the musicology of live performance, questions of authenticity in the context of repetition, and personal meaning and identity construction related to travel. Novoa's (2012) ethnography of touring musicians explores what it means to "do the road." They argues that the mobility of touring reproduces the identity of musicians. Touring is a way to validate the workplace identity of being a musician even if it is a part-time pursuit. McKinna (2014) explores what authenticity means in the context of repetition on tour. Touring involves repetitive performances in unfamiliar contexts where the artist may lack emotional connection to the audience and/or perform material by rote. McKinna concludes that authenticity is related to the experience of live music in the moment of performance with the audience. Ramella (2018) considers how musicians think of home and away when they tour. In fact, they often view the road as a home and in spite of its itinerancy, the binary of home and away collapses on tour. While this research focuses on cultural, musicological, and personal experiences of touring, I seek to fill a gap through a materialist analysis of touring as a form of wage-earning work affected by structural conditions in the music and broader economy. Under the terms of the new music industry, both working and elite musicians rely on touring for their livelihoods. It is therefore crucial to investigate the material conditions of life on the road.

3   Precariousness on Tour

The following sections will consider five themes from this research. (1) The pressure and need stay on tour; (2) insecurities related to the logistics of booking tours; (3) insecurities experienced through income composition, contract negotiation, and the costs of touring; (4) the challenges of self-care on tour; and (5) the complex and often contradictory forms of socialization on tour. This section draws from the experience of three independent touring musicians. These participants were chosen from a larger study of the touring music industry as they reflect the experiences of the broader sample (n = 40). Each informant lives and works primarily in the United States; however, they all have some international touring experience. While the paper draws on insights from the larger sample, these three cases are illustrative and representative of more generalizable observations. These narrower biographical accounts from the larger sample introduce passionate and personal testimony about the experience of touring, painting a deeper picture of life on the road than would analyzing the wider set of participants. For a broader view of this sample, see Zendel (2020).

Interviews were open-ended with informants leading the discussion as much as the researcher. Interviews were recorded, transcribed, and coded by theme in Atlas.ti. The informants were assigned pseudonyms. Additional details have been obscured to protect their identity. Participants were interviewed about their experiences touring, their backgrounds in the industry, biography, and their future prospects. These musicians work at a similar scale in the industry. Their career paths take a "bottom up" approach; that is, musician who "grows their career by sharing music on the radio or performing live shows in the hopes of building an organic following of fans … [and is] driven by passion and a strong network of listeners with the hope of becoming more well-known in the music industry" (Sater, 2019, p. 108). None of them earns significantly from recording; all of them manage their own affairs with little support from record labels, and none is under any recording or performance contract. All of them are successful by their own account, and have well developed mature careers. I argue that these particular artists capture a common experience amongst professional musicians that could be considered illustrative of a working experience in the North American music industry.

Paul is a singer-songwriter in his late 20s. He has been playing music professionally for more than nine years. He chose to pursue a music career after struggling through a STEM degree. Paul describes his music as "folk with an indie rock sensibility." Paul performs solo and as the front person of a band. While he primarily plays solo, his band accompanies him on higher profile or better paying gigs. While he tours nationally and internationally, the band rarely travels outside their home state. He would prefer to always play with a band; however, "it's more mouths to feed." Since becoming a musician, Paul has experienced some amount of local success. He has sold out a number of 200–500 person theaters as a headlining artist. He has also sold thousands of copies of his independently produced albums. He describes his greatest accomplishment as his most recent album release party where he hired a string section and backup singers to accompany him and his band through a full performance of the new album. This show, like others that Paul has promoted, is a meeting point for similar artists and like-minded audiences. Paul plays a crucial role in his local music scene. His concerts involve auditioning and hiring opening acts, promotion, bringing together numerous intermediaries, and selling merchandise and records. However, while he organizes, promotes, and plays at numerous shows over the year, these constitute only a small portion of his income. Rather, the majority of Paul's income comes from solo touring across North America and Europe.

Raoul is a solo touring artist who performs as a one-man band. He has worked as a professional musician for at least 15 years. He has a complicated guitar centered set up with effects pedals, foot-based percussion, and a looping system. Raoul is able to record these instruments as he performs and play them back in real time to create a complex layered rhythmic performance. The ephemerality of Raoul's music largely precludes him from recording. Raoul has played in bands; however, he prefers to work solo as it offers more security and less dependence on other people. His income is almost entirely from live performance. Raoul has an exhaustive resume. He has opened for high-profile artists like David Byrne, Phish, and Ani DiFranco, and has performed at large music festivals in excess of 20,000 people. However, for most of the year he plays at clubs and ski resorts, often as an opening act or as background music.

Patti is a solo singer-songwriter and the front woman of a four-piece indie rock band. She has been playing music professionally for more than ten years. Over her career, she has released solo albums, albums with her band, and collaborated as a supporting musician on other people's records. She has toured extensively as a solo artist, a front person, and as a supporting musician. She has also toured as a non-musician crew member selling and managing merchandise for other artists. Recently, Patti purchased a bus which has been converted for touring, complete with a bed and space to store instruments. Patti's case illustrates a number of salient points on how musicians earn income by living in mobile housing, working multiple jobs within the industry, having multiple creative outlets, and touring constantly in order to earn a living.

3.1 *The Pressure to Stay on Tour*

Live performance and particularly touring are important steps in a musician's career trajectories (Ballico, 2013). Both push and pull factors pressure musicians to tour more often and for longer stretches. Push factors include the cost of rent and living expenses and/or the inability to find work in saturated local music scenes. Therefore, musicians are pulled onto the road to find new markets to cultivate audiences, earn additional income, and for the joy of travel.

Raoul describes himself, as the cliché goes, as the hardest working guy in the industry. Raoul plays more than 300 gigs a year, often twice in one day. These are not two different sets; rather, he will play an early set at one venue, pack up, and drive to the next. Out of all the participants in this research, Raoul performed the most shows annually. As he recalls, "this weekend, I had an early restaurant gig Saturday morning and then I go play at night somewhere else. I was on stage for eight hours and slept for four hours." Raoul's work is labor intensive. He drives from venue to venue, carrying his equipment from show to show. In order to earn a living, Raoul must constantly be playing and booking shows. This work-life arrangement requires both the physical labor of driving, carrying equipment and performing, combined with the emotional labor of performing, booking shows, and negotiating contracts.

The individualized nature of this work adds a second dimension of precarity where Raoul experiences personal dissatisfaction when he takes time off. If he isn't working, he frames time off as losing money:

> A few years ago, I took a vacation for the first time. I went to Thailand for a month, but when I got back from that I'd been gone for a month. That was a month of gigs that I missed. Then because I was in another country, I couldn't be booking shows in advance. So that was another month in the future of shows that were not booked. That was two months of work. Then the preparation [booking more shows] turned into almost three months, a quarter of the year I lost. [Taking a vacation] was a huge damage to my career. I lost a bunch of markets and a bunch of places I was playing because I've been out of the loop. So it's like you can't take breaks.

It is important for Raoul to keep a constant pace of touring. Taking breaks means losing shows both in the present and in the future. Furthermore, success in one locality is often related to past performance. Many artists describe the need for "exposure" in order to cultivate a local fan base. Paul describes how when he first plays in a particular city, he is willing to take a loss in order to book better paying shows in the future. Both Paul and Raoul talk about markets "drying up" if they haven't traveled there recently. As such, there is a lot of pressure on musicians to cultivate fan bases and professional networks in places they tour for the prospect of future work. This complicated entrepreneurial temporality requires negotiating present wages and working conditions with future opportunities. Paul has a number of survival strategies to help navigate new markets:

> It's tough to make money as an original musician, especially going into a new market. Usually you are expecting to take a loss or maybe break even the first few times. I supplement by playing breweries or coffee shops or places like restaurants, where I don't even play any original music just so that I can be sure that I'm going to be able to afford gas and food through the majority of the trip.

Paul's touring strategy is buttressed through either playing covers or busking. If he is not driving or performing in a formal setting, he will play on the street and in parks: "[busking] is a sustainable lifestyle, especially during the summer. You can make a decent amount of money on the streets. I actually started as a busker. I've busked domestically and abroad. You can make between $10 and $20 an hour playing on the streets."

The need to perform is structured both by larger changes in the music industry, but also by changing urban and cultural economies. For Patti, time off the road means paying rent. When she is not on the road, she struggles to live in a rapidly gentrifying city. Early in her career, she sublet her apartment while she toured. However, increasingly she is more on the road than she is at home, making managing an apartment more challenging. Recently, she has been "homeless," living out of her tour bus when she is not on tour: "I came [home], where I have lived for the last nine years. The rent market had exploded. I had been living out of my bus all summer, and there was just nowhere that I could afford to live."

Patty would go on to spend the remainder of the year living out of her tour bus, effectively shifting her lifestyle to tour indefinitely. For many, committing to being a professional musician is a commitment to tour. This means relinquishing many of the foundational elements of daily life, including having a fixed address to call home. Since musicians are increasingly earning income on tour, it means that staying put or settling down means not making money, and that the expenses of daily life start to add up. Each of the musicians has varying experiences with "homelessness." All of them include the money they save on rent in the accounting of a tour's financial success. With average rents increasing across North American cities, particularly in cities with vibrant music and arts economies, combined with the changing music economy, musicians are increasingly living on the road, away from their families, support networks, and absent from local music scenes.

3.2   *Logistical Precarity*

Booking a tour is a complex process. It requires numerous business and social skills, careful planning, emotional labor, and complex legal knowledge of different jurisdictions. Booking relies on a number of networking skills, including demonstrating both social and emotional connection to the venues. Some jurisdictions have bylaws and restrictions that can limit the time and place of music, noise, alcohol and venue licensing, and more. Some jurisdictions may have parking and vehicle restrictions limiting the ability to park a tour bus or sleep in a vehicle. There may be unexpected fees at toll booths, or local taxes on fees and income.

Booking is time-consuming and unremunerated. While there are professional booking agents and tour managers which sort out the planning and execution of a tour, these intermediaries are costly and often only work with acts who can afford their services. The three musicians discussed all book shows independently and managed their own tours. They represent themselves in all their business dealings, including negotiating contracts, applying for visas, paying taxes, publishing their music, collecting royalties, and promoting their work. Booking tours also means planning contingencies such as cancelations, payments, vehicle breakdowns, and health issues. Musicians navigate numerous logistical insecurities when planning and booking tours.

Each of the artists has different approaches to how they begin the process of booking a tour. Raoul and Paul start by finding music festivals which anchor their tours. Festivals are known to pay better than one-off gigs as typically they pay a guaranteed fee. Having a "guarantee" allows artists to plan costs and other details, such as gas and driving time for the rest of the tour. Generally, this process can take months and even longer for confirmations. From there Paul says booking shows in between these dates takes

> an incredible amount of time, at least on the front end. If only it were so easy to just call someone up and say, "Hey, can I play on this date." And they say "yes." But it's all emails, I don't usually use a phone, I just send hundreds of emails out in a particular city. My strategy is to choose where you're

going, a basic routing. So you have an idea: "I'm leaving on this date, I'm coming back on this date."

Paul has to map out the rough path before he is able to start finding specific venues to play in. Once he knows the path, he searches within a drivable radius to find venues and then

> I google bars and venues. I figure out how big each one is. I look at their website and see what sort of music is playing there just to make sure that it's not like a punk or metal bar or something like that. Then I send an email to all of them with my date range, and my music, and a little bio.

Rarely is Paul the sole artist performing in a night. On many occasions, he will be slotted into an existing line up. Or, as is often the case, Paul is expected to book other artists to perform along with him in order to fill out the room.

> If it's a bigger city, I have to figure out who I'm going to play with. I have to think that if I can bring 50 people I'm going to try and get to a venue that holds like 150 people, and then I hook up with a couple other local musicians to fill out the room. If it's going to be a big gig then I research and write every musician who is in my genre and about my level. I try to build a bill.

Paul's booking process shows how artists themselves occupy complex intermediary positions in music scenes. While many venues employ dedicated bookers and promoters, frequently touring artists themselves are doing the work of producing and promoting the show. Even after a confirmation, shows can get canceled, venues close, and promoters go out of business. This is particularly salient in the COVID-19 era, as around the world, touring artists had their shows canceled with no sense of when they could reschedule and get back on the road. Few working-class artists and the venues they play in carry insurance to cover these unexpected cancelations. Of the numerous risks and contingencies that musicians face on the road, cancelations are amongst the most costly. Paul describes how as many as one in five shows he plans on a tour get canceled. A cancelation means he loses income and has to cover the costs of accommodation, food, gas, and other expenses. Some of the largest expenses on the road relate to gas, vehicle repair, and driving.

Touring musicians have intimate relationships with their vehicles. All three spend considerable time living in their touring vehicles. Patti is perhaps most comfortable in her converted bus she named *Stella*: "she's a retired 14 passenger airport shuttle bus with 430,000 miles on her." The financial success of the tour depends on *Stella*. Sleeping in the bus reduces the cost of living. *Stella* can be driven overnight with band members alternating between sleeping and driving, greatly expanding their travel range. Patti and her band will drive overnight to make a performance on time. On one occasion, they "drove straight through from Tucson to Shreveport, Louisiana. We didn't stop for 23 hours except to eat and go to the bathroom."

For Patti, a typical tour lasts four to six weeks. The whole band travels in the bus. The band had completed six of these tours in the past year to promote their new album. As Patti describes, "it was a lot of touring. I went into some pretty significant debt. We would mostly break even on tours except for bus repairs. But, over the publicity campaign and the expenses of releasing the album, I went into some debt."

She had been on the road so long that she made the decision to move out of her apartment prior to embarking on the tours. For many musicians, the cost-benefit analysis of touring carefully balances money not spent on rent while they are away. Moving out is one way to avoid paying rent and thus reduce the costs of touring. Some touring workers will keep an apartment and sublet it while they are on the road. Some, as in the case of Patti, simply plan back-to-back tours and rarely ever come off the road. In Patti's case, she decided to move out and when she comes off the road, she'll either live in the tour bus or move back in with her parents as she figures out where to go next.

3.3   Income Insecurity

Musicians get paid to perform in a number of ways, ranging from playing for so-called exposure where artists play for the hope of future work or for tips by "passing the hat" where audience members pay in tips. More formal deals include receiving a percentage of the door (ticket) and alcohol sales, or having minimum guarantees to be paid without any contingencies. Many artists also earn a living through direct merchandise sales to their fans. The risk and contingency associated with getting paid for performance is amplified through touring. Each venue and performance can have an individually negotiated contract, with multiple contingencies related to local conditions that depend on factors outside the control of musicians.

Over the course of his career, Raoul has contended with many different sources of income. When he first graduated music school, he would perform at bars and restaurants for $50 per set. However, as he started to play in bigger clubs, he was offered a percentage of door and drink sales. This means that his wage is contingent upon how many people pay to see the show. As an opening act, his percentage was comparatively small. On larger shows, these arrangements can work out well. However, many times he was let down by a promoter who failed to draw a crowd. More often, Raoul would "pass the hat" asking the audience for money directly. Some nights this worked out well. On others he might not even earn the gas money spent getting there. Therefore, Raoul says:

> I never do door deals anymore. I never take percentages of anything anymore. A lot of venues try to push you to do the door deals. I'll just not play there. I'll find something else, somebody else is going to book me on that night if you don't. Most gigs like that you lose, you always lose, there's no way you're going to win. It's a deadly game.

Unlike Raoul, Paul earns income through the sale of merchandise. As such, he is willing to accept a door deal if it means being able to sell merchandise to the audience:

> If I'm coming to a town and I have a draw, I can usually work out a door deal, and that'll be okay because a lot of my money comes from merch. So there is an impetus to continually create new stuff to push it when you're out there. I make my own t-shirts by hand with bleach and a stencil.

Paul's work as a musician is multi-faceted with him making his own merchandise to sell to his fans. This novel approach offers flexibility when negotiating contracts, as he can accept riskier and contingent gigs, provided he can sell merchandise.

As his career developed, Raoul earned bargaining power and is now able to negotiate better guarantees for his shows. However, it is a constant challenge to have to calculate and negotiate his rates:

> I try to look at it by the distance. If I'm going farther then I have to charge a little bit more. But at the same time, the farther I go, the less power I have to draw and my name isn't as well known. The farther away I go my ability

to pull more money is lowered. So there's sort of like a bell curve at which you hit the outside arc of the logic of how far to travel and where the money is going to be strong enough.

Negotiating rates is a perennial challenge. Above, Raoul discusses the challenge of balancing the expense of playing in new and more distant markets against the lower guarantees he is offered the first time he plays in a venue. This serves as a barrier where he frequently has to tour in areas where he has a reputation because new regions are both more expensive to travel to and pay less.

As a band leader, Patti faces the challenge of both booking shows and paying her bandmates. While her bandmates are sympathetic to the thin profit margins in touring, they are not volunteering to play in the band:

> The first tour I brought my band out, we were trying to get to Seattle. But, we didn't have any money until we got there. We had gigs where we were playing for tips so we were just barely covering the gas that we needed to get there. When we got there, the venue was really generous with us and kicked us an extra couple hundred bucks that they hadn't guaranteed. That was one of the few things that made the tour a financial success. We definitely did better than break even on that tour, and I was able to pay my band members like 400 bucks or something for that run. This is great. Like, if you're making 200 bucks a week, it's not a great wage, but when you're putting gas into a bus and taking care of four people on the road, it feels pretty good.

While the unexpected payout helped support the tour, the more common scenario is the unexpected expenses during the tour. Patti continues:

> We had other tours where we had to replace brake rotors in the middle of the tour. I had to take that hit and say, "okay, guys, that's not coming out of the expenses for the tour, because if it did, none of us would make any money." The rough part is making those decisions "what's going to come out of expenses?"

Other costs can be anticipated but serve as barriers to touring. For example, Patti describes how toll roads in the Eastern United States can cut into their bottom line:

> And that's when all the tolls hit. We had to pay like $28 at every toll. Coming into Pittsburgh, they wanted to charge us $28 for the toll and we barely had

any cash left. So we pulled out like our last dollar bill. We were counting out pennies. That can break us... a five day stretch where you make $20 a gig and you're not covering your gas money and you're paying like, a couple hundred dollars in tolls to get through. Cities like that can break your whole tour.

Touring economics depend on sound logistics. Any small issue such as vehicle trouble, tolls, and traffic can cost money and create delays. These artists describe times when they had to cancel shows because a small delay on the road made them late for the next show. Many artists make risky decisions around driving faster and without sleep to make up for lost time. For Paul, his income from touring is contingent on his car:

> The first couple tours I went on I made money. The last one was a pretty big loss. I actually very unfortunately had a breakdown. My transmission went out on my little Honda Civic. So in the three or so days it took me to figure that out, I had to cancel some dates. I had to rent a car for the rest of the dates. I think the most I've made on a month-long tour was like $2500, and then the least I've made is like $500 or something.

This section shows the myriad financial risks musicians face on tour. Earnings vary greatly from show to show. The way that artists get paid varies greatly. Touring is as much about earning money as it is about traveling lean and avoiding risks. While traveling in a bus has helped Patti cut costs, it occasionally exposes her band to unexpected costs. A small expense such as vehicle maintenance can greatly reduce the earnings of a touring musician.

3.4 The Toll of Constant Travel

Employment related geographic mobility generates health issues for workers, many of which are related to basic self-care (Neis et al., 2018). Touring musicians face daily problems of where and when to sleep, eat, and shower (Zendel, 2020). Some musicians tour alone, sleeping in their cars. Others tour in sleeper buses with professional drivers and rent hotel rooms. Some artists have so-called riders in their contracts that require promoters to provide healthy food and other amenities while others rely on truck stops, fast food, or cooking on camping stoves. These three artists work in the more precarious end of the spectrum. They all tour in personal vehicles, often sleeping and living in them. They all drive themselves and cook for themselves. Basic hygiene can be a challenge, as days or weeks can go by without having access to a full shower. While it is accepted in the industry that touring has rough elements, the naturalization of this experience has meant that musicians internalize precariousness as a necessary part of their career (Umney & Kretsos, 2015).

Aside from the challenge of finding performance opportunities, Paul also faces the nightly challenge of finding places to sleep, park, bathe, and eat. Paul has slept many nights in his car. He has stories about police waking him up and telling him to move along and times when people tried to break into his car while he was sleeping in it. A number of participants suggested that Walmart parking lots are the safest choice if you need to sleep overnight in a vehicle. Following a similar logic, Paul keeps a membership to a regional chain of 24-hour gyms so he can access showers as he travels. As he describes:

> Some people do the Walmart parking lot...I don't really like sleeping at rest stops. That kind of creeps me out. But I've done it a few times, covering my face with a sleeping bag...I'll usually sleep at a 24 Hour Fitness parking lot. I'm a member which allows me to have a place to sleep and I can shower and work out every day.

Paul's situation is not unique. A number of participants have experience sleeping in public parking lots and using fitness centers for bathing. Many in the research describe their move into a purpose-built tour bus as a benchmark of success.

It is important for Raoul to keep a constant pace of touring. Taking breaks means losing shows both in the present and in the future. Over winter, his tours follow a circuit of ski hills along the Rocky Mountains, over the summer he travels farther across the United States taking opportunities as they come. He tours alone in his car, sleeping overnight much the way Paul does. Raoul is used to sleeping in his car:

> I've been in a Ford Focus for two years, I get real comfortable with how to sleep in the thing. I get better sleep in the car, like in the front seat of my car, than I do in a bed. I'm so used to it. I can set it up to how I like it.

Patti and her band face the challenge of finding places for them to sleep each night. As their bus can only accommodate two comfortably, they try to find friends or fans willing to put up two of them each night. On special occasions, they will book a hotel room:

> When this is my night to spend the money on a hotel, it's going to be like the night that I get to have a little bit of "turn myself off time." Now, this is going to be my night in the middle of the tour where I just like recharge. We don't stay with friends and we spend that money. Even if it just happens like once in the middle of a two and a half or three-week tour, that's huge. That can keep me going for another week and a half.

As Americans, all three musicians struggle with health insurance. Raoul does not have health insurance. He plans his activities on tour to avoid any health risks or injuries. While he regularly plays at ski resorts, which offer the added benefit of a complimentary lift ticket and rental equipment, he never actually uses this perk because of the inherent risk to his ability to work as a musician. A small injury to his hand or wrist can stop him from playing for weeks. The cost of a hospital visit only furthers Raoul's precarious position: "I don't have health insurance. I just know that if I break an arm, I'm going to be homeless. I can't make a living, you know? So it's just not worth the risk."

Patti at the time had access to health insurance through the Medicaid expansion of the Affordable Care Act, known colloquially as Obamacare. However, she fears she'll lose her healthcare if these programs are repealed:

> Well, so far, they haven't succeeded in repealing it. So I'm just crossing my fingers on that one. Right now, I'm lucky and healthy. If I were to lose my health care, I would probably do what I did before I was on Medicaid, which was to not have any health care and continue to be a musician.

For these musicians, staying healthy is key. However, the basic elements of a healthy lifestyle—eating nutritious food and a full night's sleep, are constant challenges. For Paul, meal planning is one of the most challenging parts of touring:

> What I normally do is plan my meals around what venues will feed me. So if I'm playing at a bar or restaurant I'll have a meal there. I always try to have non-perishable or not quickly perishable, not refrigerated food in my car. Peanut butter and honey sandwiches. I do honey instead of jelly, because jelly is going to go bad. I usually take some kind of whey protein or

something just because protein is one of the hardest things to get cheaply. I try to avoid fast food.

Paul has a wide knowledge of food shelf life. For example, he keeps almond milk in his car because certain varieties do not need to be refrigerated. His knowledge of food available on the road allows him to carefully consider the calories and nutrition per dollar. Both Patti and Paul described seeking the "healthy" options at fast food places. Paul says:

> Sometimes all there is is McDonald's and Subway. If that's the case, I'll go get the grossest salad at McDonald's just to have a salad. Right? It's just this one time I'll eat fast food. Because the second that you're not supporting your body and everything goes downhill.

The toll of constant travel accumulates over a career. Irregularly sleeping in vehicles, hotels or as guests in peoples' houses is emotionally and physically exhausting for these musicians. Finding healthy food or simple care rituals like showering and exercising are a daily challenge when you need to drive long distances to get to the next show. Many musicians experience "burnout" from the work of being a professional musician, particularly the aspects associated with touring (Gross & Musgrave, 2016; Umney & Kretsos, 2015; Vaag et al., 2014).

3.5   *Crowded Isolation*

Socialization on tour is complex and features many contradictions. Bands on tour live together in close proximity for months. It can be challenging for musicians in a band to find time alone, while solo musicians spend long periods of time without meaningful human contact. While performing to an audience can be stimulating, it is in the context of work. All touring musicians experience isolation. On tour, you are away from your local scene, family, friends, and support networks. Elite artists can reproduce elements of home on tour, such as bringing family with you and traveling in luxurious tour buses. However, most musicians are traveling in crowded vans or alone in their cars.

Raoul experiences isolation and loneliness on tour. As a solo artist, he spends most of his time alone. He drives by himself to each concert. When he arrives at a show, he interacts with bar managers or venue technicians. Raoul says:

It's really fucking brutal. I could go weeks without a conversation with anybody. Being in a band is a way different experience, they're connected, everything's cool. Like, they can show up someplace. It's a group of people coming in together. When you're alone, and you show up just like "some dude showing up." It was really difficult, there's a lot of times where you're very much on my own. I had to cross some sort of mental barriers being okay with that. That was very difficult.

Touring in a band for Patti helps deal with the isolation from family and other networks. The presence of her bandmates makes her feel safe, and fills a need to be social. There is a deep camaraderie that forms between bandmates. Overtime, these relationships can become intimate and deeply personal such that being around each other can be a source of comfort and security in the context of an otherwise precarious and itinerant lifestyle. According to Patti,

there's a dynamic that develops when you're out on the road, and it's four of you. You feel attached to these people. They are a little bit of a safety net or an anchor for you. So you want alone time from other people. But you kind of want to be around them because then you have your security blanket.

While there are deep bonds, for Patti, the challenge is finding time to be alone. The constant driving in the bus combined with performing, eating, sleeping, bathing, and even taking time off together makes it hard for her and her bandmates to be alone from one another.

You also have to negotiate like, okay, "we've been around each other for two and a half weeks now. It would be great if we could all just have an hour by ourselves." Sometimes there's time for that. And you can say, "Great, let's just stop here in this park and each go our own separate ways and meet back at five." Other times [being alone] is the only thing you want, and there's no way to make it happen on that particular day.

The pace of touring and the contingent nature of tour economics means planning tours with little time off. The limited time off means more time either alone in the case of Paul and Raoul, or time sequestered with your bandmates in the case of Patti.

To save money Patti and her band try to find people to host them. Often these are friends, promoters, or even fans. Staying at people's homes involves a difficult social interaction where they must continue their performance as musicians. Often, the band member who knows the people they are staying with will feel pressure to catch up or entertain their host. Patti says:

> there was one tour that we went on where we were staying with friends every night along the way. They would be friends that one of us knew, but the other three were meeting for the first time. Whoever's friend it was, would feel a kind of pressure to want to go out and catch up and entertain them a little bit. Everyone else would get socially exhausted. So it was really important to be like, okay, it's great that we have places to stay with friends. But also, we need to balance that with how much social energy we actually have. It needs to be okay to either go camp somewhere or spend money on a hotel so that we can just be by ourselves. Or, to say to our friends like, hey, it's so great that you're willing to put us up, but we can't go out and celebrate tonight with you. Being able to set those boundaries and say, this is how much energy I have, this is where my limits are going to be. I need to stop before I get exhausted.

For the hosts, it is exciting to have their friends or a band stay with them, while for the band this is a key moment in their self-care and personal reproduction. The public nature of work in the arts means often having to perform even in private spaces, including the places you stay on tour. Musicians on tour face constant challenges to their personal space and boundaries. While performing in public is an essential part of being a musician, living in public, traveling alone or having to continue a performance as a guest complicates their work experience. These musicians face unique challenges balancing work and life, such as the pressure to be "always on" (Banks et al., 2014). Touring blurs boundaries between work and home as musicians are expected to engage in activities not normally recognized as "work," such as entertaining hosts.

4   Conclusion

This paper has presented five ways that independent or "bottom up" musicians experience precariousness on tour. Live performance often involves travel, exposing artists to numerous risks. Aside from the dangers associated with vehicle travel, musicians also experience exhaustion, isolation, and loneliness. They face daily challenges to eating healthy and getting adequate sleep. They carefully balance their quality of life on the road against their income. Touring is risky, where small, unexpected expenses such as vehicle troubles can make an entire tour unprofitable. The general precariousness that musicians face navigating booking and contract negotiations is amplified as they cross jurisdictions. Getting paid is not easy for any contractor, let alone a traveling musician. Many workers experience the exhaustion of being "always on" and "always away" in mobile architectures that blur both the temporal and spatial boundaries between work and non-work (Zendel, 2020). The experiences of musicians in this chapter represent the cutting edge of pressures affecting many workers outside of music, and lessons from these musicians are a valuable addition to gig economy literature (Haynes & Marshall, 2018). The exposure to risk on tour relates to broader changes in the music industry. Incomes and livelihoods are increasingly cobbled together around performance adjacent sources. The entrepreneurial and innovative character of musicians is often valorized to the point of fetishization (Coulson, 2012; Haynes & Marshall, 2018). Current debates around the nature of creative and cultural labor celebrate the affective dimensions of music making, while glossing over many material conditions of the people who make music (Long & Barber, 2014). Other scholars, particularly urban geographers, consider the role that musicians play in place-making, suggesting that vibrant live music scenes and supporting musicians are instrumental paths to urban growth (Florida, 2005). Ethnographic analysis of the working lives of musicians demystifies the experience of working in cultural industries and the spatial lives of musicians.

While it is difficult to make a clear throughline, suggesting that these particular artists are pushed to tour from broader technological changes, it is well documented that musicians and other workers are earning more of their living through performance and touring activities (Frith, 2013; Holt, 2010; McKinna, 2014; Tschmuck, 2017; Webster et al., 2018). Touring exposes artists to specific forms of precariousness related to travel. There is an urgent need for ethnographic inquiry to better understand the lived experience of working-class musicians. However, when scholars do attend to the everyday life of working musicians, it is generally spatially bound to specific cities and places (Hracs, 2012). Indeed, a mobile population is a challenge for any ethnographer (Cresswell et al., 2016). By focusing on the working lives of three working-class musicians, I center a common but largely unglamorous experience of work in the music industry (see also Umney & Kretsos, 2014). It is crucial for music scholars to understand the hardships and working conditions that working musicians experience every day. The working lives of musicians are temporally and geographically fragmented which increases insecurity in terms of predictability in the time and place of their work, wages for their work, the places they live and stay, and how they care for themselves and each other. All of this is manifest at the scale of the body, heightening the need to negotiate everyday life and the self in new ways.

REFERENCES

Bacache-Beauvallet, M., Bourreau, M., & Moreau, F. (2016). Information asymmetry and 360-degree contracts in the recorded music industry. *Revue d'économie Industrielle, 156,* 57–90.

Ballico, C. (2013). *Bury me deep in isolation: A cultural examination of a peripheral music industry and scene.* Doctoral dissertation, Edith Cowan University.

Banks, M., Gill, R., & Taylor, S. (2014). Introduction: Cultural work, time and trajectory. In M. Banks, R. Gill, & S. Taylor (Eds.), *Theorizing cultural work.* Routledge.

Coulson, S. (2012). Collaborating in a competitive world: Musicians' working lives and understandings of entrepreneurship. *Work Employment and Society, 26*(2), 246–261.

Cresswell, T., Dorow, S., & Roseman, S. (2016). Putting mobility theory to work: Conceptualizing employment-related geographical mobility. *Environment and Planning A: Economy and Space, 48*(9), 1787–1803.

Eriksson, M., Fleischer, R., Johansson, A., Snickars, P., & Vonderau, P. (2019). *Spotify teardown: Inside the black box of streaming music.* The MIT Press.

Florida, R. (2005). *Cities and the creative class.* Routledge.

Frith, S. (2013). Live music exchange. *Popular Music, 32*(2), 297–301.

Gill, R., & Pratt, A. (2008). In the social factory? Immaterial labour, precariousness and cultural work. *Theory, Culture & Society, 25*(7–8), 1–30.

Gross, S., & Musgrave, G. (2016). *Can music make you sick? Music and depression part 1: Pilot survey report help musicians UK.* University of Westminster/ Music Tank.

Haynes, J., & Marshall, L. (2018). Reluctant entrepreneurs: Musicians and entrepreneurship in the "new" music industry. *British Journal of Sociology, 69*(2), 459–482.

Holt, F. (2010). The economy of live music in the digital age. *European Journal of Cultural Studies, 13*(2), 243–261.

Hracs, B. J. (2012). A creative industry in transition: The rise of digitally driven independent music production. *Growth and Change, 43*(3), 442–461.

Karubian, S. (2008). 360 deals: An industry reaction to the devaluation of recorded music note. *Southern California Interdisciplinary Law Journal, 18*(2), 395–462.

Long, P., & Barber, S. (2014). Voicing passion: The emotional economy of song-writing. *European Journal of Cultural Studies, 18*(2), 142–157.

Marshall, L. (2013). The 360 deal and the 'new' music industry. *European Journal of Cultural Studies, 16*(1), 77–99.

McKinna, D. R. (2014). The touring musician: Repetition and authenticity in performance. *IASPM Journal, 4*(1), 56–72.

Mühlbach, S., & Arora, P. (2020). Behind the music: How labor changed for musicians through the subscription economy. *First Monday, 25*(4). https://doi.org/10.5210/fm.v25i4.10382

Neis, B., Barber, L., Fitzpatrick, K., Hanson, N., Knott, C., Premji, S., & Thorburn, E. (2018). Fragile synchronicities: Diverse, disruptive and con-straining rhythms of employment-related geographical mobility, paid and unpaid work in the Canadian context. *Gender, Place & Culture, 25*(8), 1175–1192.

Novoa, A. (2012). Musicians on the move: Mobilities and identities of a band on the road. *Mobilities, 7*(3), 349–368.

Prior, N. (2018). *Popular music, digital technology and society.* SAGE Publications.

Ramella, A. L. (2018). Deciphering movement and stasis: Touring musicians and their ambivalent imaginings of home and belonging. *International Journal of Tourism Anthropology, 6*(4), 323–339.

Sinnreich, A. (2013). *The piracy crusade: How the music industry's war on sharing destroys markets and erodes civil liberties.* University of Massachusetts Press.

Stahl, M., & Meier, L. M. (2012). The firm foundation of organizational flexibil-ity: The 360 contract in the digitalizing music industry. *Canadian Journal of Communication, 37*(3), 441.

Standing, G. (2016). *The precariat: The new dangerous class.* Bloomsbury Publishing.

Tschmuck, P. (2017). *The economics of music.* Agenda Publishing.

Umney, C., & Kretsos, L. (2014). Creative labour and collective interaction: The working lives of young jazz musicians in London. *Work, Employment & Society, 28*(4), 571–588.

Umney, C., & Kretsos, L. (2015). "That's the experience": Passion, work precar-ity, and life transitions among London jazz musicians. *Work and Occupations, 42*(3), 313–334.

Vaag, J., Giæver, F., & Bjerkeset, O. (2014). Specific demands and resources in the career of the Norwegian freelance musician. *Arts & Health, 6*(3), 205–222.

Webster, E., Brennan, M., Behr, A., Cloonan, M., & Ansell, J. (2018). *Valuing live music: The UK live music census 2017 report. Executive Summary.* Retrieved April 6, 2021, from http://uklivemusiccensus.org/wp-content/uploads/2018/03/UK-Live-Music-Census-2017-executive-summary.pdf

Wikström, P. (2014). The music industry in an age of digital distribution. In M. Castells, D. Gelernter, J. Vázquez, E. Morozov, & M. Hyppönen (Eds.), *Change: 19 key essays on how the internet is changing our lives*. Turner/ BBVA Group.

Zendel, A. M. (2020). "There are no days off, just days without shows": Precarious mobilities in the touring music industry. *Applied Mobilities, 6*, 1–18.

INDEX[1]

A
Agent of change, 19, 59
Agglomeration, 72, 78, 80, 84, 95
    See also Clusters
Album, 69, 73–83, 85, 98–108,
    105n7, 112, 113, 121, 124,
    125, 130
Anthropology, 5
Atlanta (United States), vi, 10, 94, 99,
    101, 104–106, 109, 114
Audience, 16, 21, 25, 27, 32, 46, 59,
    71, 97, 104, 105, 110, 121, 123,
    125, 126, 130, 131, 136
Austin (United States), 40
Australia, 54, 59, 69
Authenticity, 5, 6, 10, 51, 94, 97, 99,
    100, 106, 107, 110, 113, 123

B
Berlin (Germany), 75–77,
    79–81, 83, 84

Black, 49, 55, 59
Booking (of performance), 120
Branding, 24, 28, 29, 97
    See also Marketing
Buzz, 53, 109, 111, 113

C
Canada, 42, 49, 50, 55
Career (in music), 8, 10, 25, 26, 93,
    97, 100, 109, 110, 113, 124,
    125, 131
CDs, 69, 110
Census, 54, 55, 61
Centrality, 6, 10, 68–85
Charts, 69, 73, 74, 93, 95,
    98, 99, 101
Circulation, 4, 9, 40–62, 68
Class (economic), 123
Classical music, 3, 55
Clubs, 110, 111, 125, 131
    See also Theatres; Venues

---

[1] Note: Page numbers followed by 'n' refer to notes.

The manufacturer's authorised representative in the EU is Springer
Nature Customer Service Centre GmbH, Europaplatz 3, 69115 Heidelberg,
Germany. If you have any concerns regarding our products, please
contact ProductSafety@springernature.com

Printed and bound by CPI Group (UK) Ltd, Croydon, CR0 4YY
29/04/2026
02099525-0008